enough.

finding peace in a world of distractions, hustle, and expectations

by Barbara Burgess

BALBOA.PRESS
A DIVISION OF HAY HOUSE

Copyright © 2024 by Barbara Burgess.

All rights reserved. No part of this book may be used or reproduced by
any means, graphic, electronic, or mechanical, including photocopying,
recording, taping or by any information storage retrieval system
without the written permission of the author except in the case
of brief quotations embodied in critical articles and reviews.

Balboa Press books may be ordered through booksellers or by contacting:

Balboa Press
A Division of Hay House
1663 Liberty Drive
Bloomington, IN 47403
www.balboapress.com
844-682-1282

Because of the dynamic nature of the Internet, any web addresses or
links contained in this book may have changed since publication and
may no longer be valid. The views expressed in this work are solely those
of the author and do not necessarily reflect the views of the publisher,
and the publisher hereby disclaims any responsibility for them.

The author of this book does not dispense medical advice or prescribe the use
of any technique as a form of treatment for physical, emotional, or medical
problems without the advice of a physician, either directly or indirectly. The
intent of the author is only to offer information of a general nature to help
you in your quest for emotional and spiritual well-being. In the event you use
any of the information in this book for yourself, which is your constitutional
right, the author and the publisher assume no responsibility for your actions.

Any people depicted in stock imagery provided by Getty Images are
models, and such images are being used for illustrative purposes only.
Certain stock imagery © Getty Images.

Print information available on the last page.

ISBN: 979-8-7652-5603-9 (sc)
ISBN: 979-8-7652-5602-2 (hc)
ISBN: 979-8-7652-5601-5 (e)

Library of Congress Control Number: 2024920183

Balboa Press rev. date: 11/12/2024

DEDICATION

This book is dedicated to you, my dear friend, ENOUGH. Thank you for trusting me to tell our story with all its magnificent imperfections. I feel a bit shy about asking, but if you are amenable, I invite you to move in permanently. I have a vacancy in my heart with NOT ENOUGH's recent departure. Sorry if the space is a bit messy. Feel free to set the remainder of his belongings at the curb. Forever yours, Barbara.

TABLE OF CONTENTS

The insidious impostor creeps in on septic feet, ready to sever the carotid path that allows all joy and flow . . . this innocuous pseudo-helper spreads his cancerous growth through whispers, talks, shouts, and screams . . . YOU ARE NOT ENOUGH! THERE IS NOT ENOUGH. BE AFRAID, he says. I scramble, judge, hide, duck, run, spin, and beat beat beat my heart as fast as I can. I keep up the pace to dodge him . . . over and over and over until finally, in quiet resignation, his voices ARE me . . . the familiar . . . what I know . . .

. . . and yet . . . sometimes . . . something else . . . a shooting star in the darkest of nights, some small flash signals differently . . . a sweet word, a soft touch, a kind acknowledgment . . . I want to embrace it, receive it, absorb it. Instead, I run. I hit. I destroy. Because what I know is that I am deeply familiar with NOT ENOUGH. NOT ENOUGH fills me from the inside and permeates my DNA. I understand how peculiar this is, how strange that I built a walking-talking-pretending machine-like homage to NOT ENOUGH.

How did this come to be? How can I deny the proof that says otherwise, the proof presented to me in every moment in ways big and small? How did I come to perpetuate the always-starving lie? Why did I embrace the falsehood? How did I come to draw it in, seek it out, and desperately recreate it over and over?

chapter 1

NOT ENOUGH, MEET ENOUGH

WHO DO YOU THINK YOU ARE?!!!! GET A GRIP. GROW UP. GIVE UP. FORGET IT. IT'S TOO LATE. IF YOU HAD MORE TALENT OR MONEY OR BEAUTY. BESIDES, THERE IS NOT ENOUGH TO GO AROUND . . .

I learned to live in the lap of NOT ENOUGH. Perhaps you, too, live in some version of NOT ENOUGH. I do this in small ways, like comparing my thighs to others. But I can also do this in large ways, like not writing or risking, singing or dancing, showing up or speaking out.

But what if . . . what if, for one small, tiny pinprick of light opening, there were a different way? a different path? Something bigger and better and delightful and embracing?

What if I am enough, have enough, and do enough? What if everything I seek lives within and around me all the time? Okay . . . most of the time?

The Chalk Experience

On a warm June day, six months after giving notice at my job and making the choice to launch my own business, I placed a bucket of chalk on the city sidewalk in front of my home in Chicago. I wrote, "Please write and draw," and made a few colorful, shaded circles to get the ball rolling. The avalanche that followed over the months to come kept taking my breath away.

After setting out the chalk on that first day, I walked back into the house to grab my laptop and re-emerged to plunk myself in a folding chair on our front porch. As I settled in to get some work done, I heard a young boy begging his adult to stop and chalk, pleading in a tone that only young humans seem to make. I stayed out of view, my chair strategically hidden behind a potted plant in the corner of our porch, as this adorable little human insistently tugged the sleeve of his busy, phone-distracted parent. This little one pleaded to stop so they could draw and color. I heard the surrendering, begrudging exhale as the adult eventually gave in. The boy plopped himself down and got to work. I went back to my email.

After a few minutes, I heard the boy talking to himself as he colored and chalked: "Look at the blue," "Nope, I need more, more, more over here." The adult periodically joined in with sweet rhythmic acknowledgments: "Ooh, I love that color, how beautiful." After a pause that seemed to stretch and expand the fabric of time, fifteen minutes that felt like an hour, I no longer heard any sounds. I sensed that my visitors had left, and the coast was clear. I felt safe enough to peek out from my corner perch. The sidewalk was empty, and I skipped down the steps to look at what he had made. I imagined seeing a simple line drawing, the scribble of a cat or a dog that only a parent could pretend to recognize.

What I saw dragged tears from a space deep inside myself that I had long since forgotten. On top of my original colored-chalk circles, this young child had added magnificently gorgeous, brightly colored, Saturn-like rings. I could barely comprehend how he got the angle and shading just right, but he turned my optimistic little orbs into magnificent planets surrounded by stars.

What remained on my sidewalk was artwork that transported me to the feeling I had when I first saw real photographs of space—stunning, imaginative, expansive. This blessing, the sucker punch beauty of it all, hit me so hard and fast I could barely breathe. From somewhere inside me, very deep, very old, and very warm, I felt her sneak in, slowly at first, but then gradually expanding and finally enfolding me fully . . . ENOUGH. She stretched out her octopus tendrils from the center of my heart and stroked my belly. I cried and cried.

Shared Pictures on Our Hearts

This whole gift had emerged with the greatest of ease. Earlier that day, as I was cleaning off a shelf above a jumble of coats in our front closet, I stumbled across the kids' sidewalk chalk. I grabbed a large, lidded glass jar, gathering dust on the floor in our garage. I don't know what compelled me, but I had decided to open up our front sidewalk to others. Over these six months, on the way to launching my own business, the concrete of my old routine had started to crack, and the fissures were making space for planting new seeds. Moment-savoring possibilities were beginning to sprout.

I never imagined such a small gesture would birth such joy in my new daily routine. The little boy who turned circles into planets had tossed a snowball that eventually became that avalanche. I left out the sidewalk chalk and added a phrase that I regularly rewrote: "Feel free to write, draw, or scribble."

Others joined in almost daily. I'd wake up every morning to new chalk artwork. Some drawings were scribbles from kids barely old enough to hold the chalk. Others were masterpieces from clearly talented artists.

Some were professions of love for their partners, strong initials surrounded by big, optimistic hearts. Others were calls for social activism or inspirational statements about love, joy, or peace.

Like Tibetan monks clearing their painstakingly created sand mandala, Mother Nature would periodically rain down and cleanse the entire canvas. Rather than feeling sad about the erased artwork, I eagerly looked forward to the new creations waiting to be birthed from the blank slate of future passers-by. The sidewalk chalk experiment lasted long enough that I would be working out in the garden in front of the house, and someone would stop to make a comment, to thank me, or to unmask themselves. "I love that you guys do this!" or "I so enjoy looking at the chalk every time I pass by. It is so uplifting." Or "Hey, I am one of your night artists. I draw the cartoons when I'm walking home from work. Can I buy some more chalk for you?" There were also the anonymous neighbors who simply left new containers of chalk to restock the supply or the stranger who initially scared me when he pounded on the front door of our house one evening. After my shock wore off, I heard him explaining that his dog had accidentally knocked over and cracked the glass jar with the chalk, and he wanted to pay for it or buy a new one.

I felt uplifted. In a world where we seek so desperately to belong that we end up "other"-ing people who don't look like us, act like us, think like us, or vote like us, I found the chalk experience unifying and hopeful. I didn't get to know people by their titles, categories, or affiliations. I got to know them through the shared pictures in our hearts, the ones that made their way from their insides to my sidewalk. To this day, I have chats through chalk with people I never met. (Special shout out to Max and all your signed greetings. We haven't met yet, but perhaps we shall before this book is published!) The chalk opened the door to many new adventures.

The months passed, and then one day in October, I looked out the front door and saw an older man sitting on the front steps. I wondered if I needed to do something or call someone. We live in the city, and strangers on the steps usually mean a problem to handle. Eventually, I was able to position myself at an awkward angle to see through the window without being seen. I noticed that this man was accompanied by two little girls chalking while playing with the plastic Halloween skeletons I had hung in the tree.

They lingered so long that I eventually did step outside. He sheepishly apologized for staying there so long, sitting on our porch steps. He asked if it was okay. "Of course," was always the right answer at these times. The man told me he was a grandpa watching his granddaughters. His son and daughter-in-law lived down the block and had just arrived home with their newborn. For him, the steps and chalk offered a welcome respite, a way to be out of the house on a sunny day, a way to match his desire for some ease with the bubbling energy of these beautiful little beings. For me, offering a space of shared humanity was not a sacrifice but a gift. The dollar store plastic skeletons held no major significance for me but brought great value to him and his grandchildren.

By now, I was starting to get used to this warm community feeling of strangers, and the real sharing that the chalk drew out of the people who stopped. Grandpa went on to tell me how the kids had been scripting fantastic conversations between the plastic skeletons, an entire play performed on our front lawn unbeknownst to me.

Through the chalk, ENOUGH had knocked on my door and introduced herself. I knew she wanted to rent some space, but my internal community was still in committee, weighing the pros and cons. She seemed like a good addition now, but what about the future? Let's not be naive, a voice laced with skepticism shouted from somewhere in my mind. Won't it hurt much more if I lift my hopes high only to increase the possibility of a longer fall and a harder crash when I'm wrong? How will I feel if I ultimately discover that ENOUGH is simply a mirage, a fluke, a passing daydream? After all, look over there! What about what they are doing? I mean if you compare . . .

chapter 2

DEATH BY COMPARISON:
NOT ENOUGH

LOOK WHAT THEY DID . . . IF YOU WERE BETTER, YOU WOULD HAVE DONE THAT. LOOK WHAT THEY GOT . . . YOU THOUGHT ABOUT GETTING THAT . . . YOU WANTED THAT . . . IF YOU HAD BEEN SMARTER AND DONE IT EARLIER, YOU WOULD HAVE HAD THAT. YOU'LL NEVER BE AS GOOD AS THEY ARE.

I sat in the coffee shop, enjoying the fact that I had chosen to put my five-foot-three-inch, size-14 body into a pair of cream-colored vegan leather pants.

I have never worn leather pants. I have never worn cream-colored pants. My go-to uniform at this point was black, black, and more black (on an outrageous day, I might mix in some gray).

But I had earned this new experience. I had gone out to invest in some clothes that fit the body I had, not the body I fantasized about returning to. And I had selected high-quality, thoughtful garments that fit well, felt good to wear, and were well-made. ENOUGH snuck her way into my wardrobe, and I felt an unexpected long-desired sense of joy.

But then SHE walked in. Damn her in her cream-colored vegan leather pants with the stick-thin legs that scream, "I travel to Paris regularly and am often mistaken for a local who just attended the opera." In the blink of an eye (Seriously?!), NOT ENOUGH shoved me into the pit of despair . . . the black tar-filled space where comparison creeps in, and hip checks ENOUGH so NOT ENOUGH can claim his territory.

Comparison kills. Plain and simple.

Little c vs. Big C Comparison

I guess I should explain. I'm talking about the big C comparison, not the little c comparison.

With "little c" comparisons, I might notice the difference between variables to adjust. I might notice that the floor is a little higher over here vs. over there. I pay attention so that I don't accidentally trip. Or I might notice that I like their presentation style better than mine, so I change mine to better match that version. Or I might be selecting between two job offers, and it's helpful to compare the variables to assess my preferences. Those are all "little c" comparisons.

The big C comparison, on the other hand, carries along an unmistakable sinking stomach potion formula. After making a big C comparison, I feel less than. Rather than my heart expanding, lifting me up, and holding possibilities, I feel a little smaller, a little less worthy, a little visit from NOT ENOUGH.

By its very nature, comparison pulls out an enormous megaphone, loudspeaker, football field-sized video screen, and broadcasts to me: YOU ARE NOT ENOUGH.

Any time I get comfortable or have a moment of ease, I think maybe, just maybe, this time, maybe I am okay. But I glance up and see THEM or HER or HIM—some in-person walking monument to "better than me." I compare myself to someone or something, and when I do, I am able to completely obliterate any internal sense of value.

I may simply compare my feet to their feet. But even that tiny comparison, that droplet of a virus, gains a foothold that infects my entire being.

I compare big things: their career, their finances, their car, their home, their wardrobe, their intelligence, or their connections.

Big or small, I harm myself by the big C comparisons I make. As a kid on vacation, I once saw a Henry Dyke quote on a postcard in a souvenir shop. I cried on the inside reading the words.

"Use what talents you possess; The woods would be very silent if no birds sang there except those that sang best."

At that time in my life, at the awkward age of twelve, I liked to sing. Sadly, I had already decided I could never be an amazing singer. I had seen and heard so many people with beautiful voices that I decided I wasn't good enough to join those ranks. As a pre-teen, I already restricted my concert venues to the shower.

The Ladder of Comparison

At that ripe young age, I had already learned about the ladder of comparison. Do you know the ladder I'm talking about? It stretches for miles upon miles. Let me explain.

Imagine a ladder with feet planted on the earth that reaches way up into the sky. Every ladder rung only holds one person. When it comes to singing, I probably stood on a ladder rung somewhere in the middle to the bottom half. I could carry a tune, hit some notes, and enjoy singing. But when I glanced up the ladder to the people I knew standing above me at age 12, I couldn't even see the top. The amazing girl in the high school musical? Fifty rungs up. The person singing on TV? Thousands of rungs up. The top rungs of the ladder? Today I can't even imagine all the humans who live up there—gospel singers for sure, rappers-yes, opera singers-definitely—and so many wonderful humans that own their own categories: Whitney Houston, Aretha Franklin, Janis Joplin, Louis Armstrong, Beyoncé, Lady Gaga, Mavis Staples, Johnny Cash, Pink. I would lose count if I even tried.

And that's just singing. What about other ladder categories? Like business success ladders?

I coached an executive. Let's call her Taylor. Taylor referred another executive to me, Lila. Taylor both admired and felt jealous of all of Lila's achievements. Lila had attended the best preparatory and Ivy League schools, worked for one of the most prestigious consulting firms, traveled around the world, and made significant money in a family business.

When I began coaching Lila, I spent our first session listening to her life story. We were looking for themes that began in early life so we could make small adjustments and steer her ship in the direction she wanted. Taylor had been right about Lila. Lila had achieved all of the things Taylor envied. I heard the details of her upbringing, her travel, her access to international friends, the private prep boarding school she attended, and so on.

But do you know what Lila felt most challenged by? The main thing she wanted to address? Comparison! Lila compared herself to still another friend, Ramona. Ramona had made a killing in the markets in her early 30s and had reached a significant level of wealth before she was 35. Ramona had attended a slightly better Ivy League school than Lila. Lila's admiration and jealousy of Ramona were as strong, or stronger, than Taylor's for Lila.

These three strong female executives were all wildly successful by most standards. They all made excellent livings, had loving partners, and lived in beautiful homes they owned. At the very same time, each one of them stood on a rung of the ladder of comparison. They each lived with a state of unworthiness that was exacerbated by constantly looking up the ladder to the person who, in their opinion, had really made it and who stood on a rung of the ladder above them.

A Ladder of Wealth

Probably the biggest ladder of comparison we climb and hang on to for dear life is the ladder of wealth. I know this ladder exists because I have supported many, many people now, and everyone talks about it without ever naming it directly.

A relative of mine came into some significant money. In relative terms, you can imagine that this money would represent the equivalent of a big lottery jackpot. He took me to lunch (and, to his credit, being very self-aware, sheepishly made the following comment). He said, "Do you know that, compared to most of the people I am around now, I am actually not very wealthy?"

Wow! That struck me hard. I fantasized about how happy I'd be and what I'd do if I had won a lottery jackpot equivalent to his payout. But when he made this money, he simply moved up to an entirely new section of the ladder that most of us don't even know exists. And in his perception of that section of the ladder, he hung on toward the bottom. What?!!!!

Looking Down the Ladder

And although looking up the ladder causes constant problems, looking down the ladder doesn't work either. Looking down takes many forms. I may feel insecure looking up the ladder, so I comfort myself by glancing down to see how much better I am than others, piling some false superiority on top of my inferiority. I have learned this about myself over and over. When I look down my nose at someone else, I usually feel insecure. I try, usually without noticing, to feel superior to anybody or anything just to comfort myself.

But that's not my only problem when looking down the ladder. I may genuinely feel superior to those below me, which causes me to pity them. This is a false sense of sympathy that is nothing more than another version of my inferiority disguised in a do-gooder cloak. Yikes!

A Closer Look at the Ladder

Let's take a closer look at this ladder. The ladder feet are firmly planted on the earth. Again, only one person gets to live on any one rung.

Imagine the billions of people on the planet all stacked up with one rung per person.

Imagine, if you can, the full height of this ladder. If you travel from the very bottom of this ladder to the very top, you realize that the ladder keeps going and going and going. The ladder appears to go on infinitely, but perhaps you'd eventually reach the top in a plane or even a spaceship. At the top of the ladder is *only one spot*—room for one person to stand.

So, you can spend your entire life in a repetitive cycle of comparing, competing, and climbing, comparing, competing, and climbing. But out of the billions of humans on the planet, and the countless others who have passed on—only one person technically gets to live at the top of that ladder. Let's imagine the ladder represents financial wealth. You only have one wealthiest person on the planet at any given time.

But wait, there's more!

Your ladder may not exactly match someone else's ladder. You may envision someone at the top of your ladder, but in their mind, someone else probably lives on the rung above them. Maybe they know they are the wealthiest person in their entire life but compared to someone else's stunning good looks or loving relationship, they place themselves lower on the ladder of comparison. For them, money becomes irrelevant as they compare themselves to people with better looks or enduring love.

And there's still more!

If a person feels they have reached the top rung (so far, I haven't met this human), they can't rest there because any little breeze, any tiny shift of unwanted circumstances pushes them off that rung. That slight change could force them to surrender that top spot to someone else.

Are you the wealthiest person alive? An extraordinary wind of market changes can quickly blow some of your wealth away while increasing someone else's portfolio. The most gorgeous person on the planet? Natural aging or a car accident could push you right off that rung.

Solving the Ladder Problem

So, how do we solve the problem of the ladder? Easy. We don't. Just get off the ladder! Make no mistake. Your vacation off the ladder will likely not last forever. Mine certainly hasn't. I have yet to meet the person who has permanently removed themselves. Maybe the Dalai Lama, but we haven't met . . . Yet. (BTW-I am very, very open to that introduction by anyone at any time; it would be an honor.) Personally, I still catch myself climbing on a rung pretty regularly, but I know that I can develop tremendous muscles as I learn to step off.

My job now? Notice when the ladder's magnetic pull draws me toward it and away from an increasing sense of self-acceptance. This pull of the ladder reminds me of my relationship with my fridge. Sometimes, I just find myself standing in front of the fridge, door hanging open, jaw hanging slack, looking longingly into its cold belly. I don't exactly remember walking to the kitchen or opening the door, but there I am, nonetheless. I have experienced the same thing with the ladder.

I left the house for the day feeling happy and valuable, saw someone beautiful who seemed more successful, and Damnit! There I am on the ladder again.

No harm. No foul. When this happens, I can notice it, release the white-knuckled grip on the rails, and step off.

Off the Ladder = Having More of What We Want

Don't confuse stepping off the ladder with not being ambitious. I find that people are more ambitious and take more risks when they are not on the ladder. I think that when we step off, we take back all the energy we spent gripping and climbing the ladder and do something magnificently, wonderfully, satisfyingly different with it. Things like: build a business, write a song, fill a garden with vegetables, or learn about investing. You may even have time to ride a bike! Think of what it may mean to make more space in your day (or mind). Perhaps you'd like to lead a company in an unapologetic style that is all your own? Maybe you decide to help a person who needs it. Maybe you apologize instead of defending yourself. You may find that you begin (once off the ladder) to smile more, to be outrageous, or to have the courage to tell someone they matter to you.

When you step off the ladder, you open up endless space to do whatever the f*ck you want. You may be surprised to find that you choose to do the exact same things you are doing now. I do a lot of that. Instead of suffering through my life and the choices I make, instead of constantly ranking my life progress against others, I can now increasingly enjoy what I am doing. I may be doing a lot of the same things, but I am doing them for myself, not to reach the next rung of the ladder.

An Alternate Reality

Let's be outrageous and consider, what if we couldn't compare?

What if—for a tiny brief speck of a pause—we saw a different way? A different path? Something bigger and better and delightful and embracing?

What if we exited the womb and entered the world without the ability to compare?

What if we walked around the world as stupid idiots, wonderfully stupid and joyous idiots. I know this won't happen in our lifetimes, but I have fun thinking about how we might behave differently (and have more fun).

I haven't yet taken the stage to sing because I'm not "good" compared to others. But If I had been birthed without a comparison gene, I'm relatively sure I'd be starring in my own supremely cheesy musical. What risks might I have taken early on in my business career if I had never worried about others thinking less of me, when compared to someone else? And would I actually enjoy going to the beach, no matter the size or shape of my body? I don't know, but a girl can dream!

We probably can't eliminate comparison. And at the highest level, comparison in the right dose delivers beautiful value. But for me, my overused comparison muscle deepens the neural superhighways that NOT ENOUGH loves to speed surf.

Think back to the ladder. Very few people in the world will ever be at the absolute top. I don't mean the "top 10" top, but the absolute number one position on the top of anything. And, even if they do, they absolutely won't be at the top of every "best" list. That means that each and every one of us always, *always, always,* has someone better than us at any one thing.

For many of us, comparison, when overused, can lead to depression and anxiety. Actually, I should probably say that I get anxious and depressed when I overly focus on comparing myself to others. So, I prefer not to do it. Outrageous, I know. Impossible, probably. But these days, I prefer to spend the energy I would use comparing in other ways.

But Wait! The Benefit of Comparison

You may say, "I love when others do better than me. Comparison serves me!" Or you may say, "I'm a competitive tennis athlete, and I compare myself to those better than me to improve myself and my game. I work my tail off and reduce my gaps to win the next match. What is wrong with that?"

Easy answer. Nothing. Absolutely nothing is wrong with that. If you revel when others do better than you, I am giving you a high-five and a fast pass to skip this section of the book. I don't use comparisons that way most of the time. I am working to increasingly celebrate and learn from others who are better than me, and I think that might be as close as I get. I do love to watch two very classy, well-valued competitors go at it. They leave it all on the court in their competition, and at the end of the day, they shake hands, fist bump, bow, or hug right after the match . . . after one lost and one won. They respect each other because they know that, on any given day, the roles might reverse. Those demonstrations of respect move me to tears.

Maybe you don't fall into any of these characterizations and are more of the "I'll win at all costs, even if it means crushing you" type. I recognize your choice. I recognize your right to exist. But you are not my people, and I choose to hang out in different circles. (See Chapter 3: Change as an Option, Not an Imperative.)

Talking about the Reality vs. Living the Reality

"I sold three more packages." "I have twelve new clients." "I got a 40% increase with the promotion." "I created my own course." Many people I had previously coached, encouraged, cheered on, and sometimes even given free support to, succeeded beyond what I could have imagined before ENOUGH introduced herself to me. These clients had envisioned their success, done the work, applied it, sought out resources, and believed in themselves. I also had a front-row seat supporting them from their beginning vision(s) to witness their clear results. If I had been aware of the fact that ENOUGH was sitting next to me in every moment, I would hear and see her sing, dance, and shout, "See! I told you. Just believing matters. Look what a difference you made. They are making money and having success, and you helped create that by visioning, contributing, and coaching. Congrats!"

So, I still sometimes feel the acid burn in my stomach—scarcity, jealousy, inferiority, superiority covering inferiority, fear—NOT ENOUGH. I wonder, how the hell did I let him into all these interactions? I am writing a book about ENOUGH, after all. I know better, and yet I still periodically see NOT ENOUGH sitting there when someone else achieves—even if I helped them achieve. Rather than being excited about their wins, I sometimes feel that green serpent of envy rear its head. In my darkest times, I feel like I have lost ENOUGH. But she never leaves. ENOUGH always lives in my heart. Even as I type this, she pokes my ribs, reminding me that I am allowed to be human.

———

In the end, I am continually discovering. If I want to have a magnificent life, a wealthy life, career success, and creative expression, I need to stop comparing and do what moves me. I have to stop wasting my energy climbing the ladder. I need to step off, rest, and play. When I do, miracles wait in the wings.

————

remember:

Comparison kills dreams, joy, and possibilities.

CHAPTER 3

CHANGE AS AN OPTION, NOT AN IMPERATIVE: ENOUGH

LOOK YOUNGER. GET A FASTER CAR. LOSE WEIGHT. MEDITATE. MAKE MILLIONS. UPGRADE YOUR HOUSE. GET ANOTHER HOUSE. BE HEALTHY. BE CONSCIOUS. BE A BETTER FRIEND, PARENT, SIBLING, CITIZEN. FIX THE WORLD. THEY NEED TO CHANGE. YOU NEED TO CHANGE. WE ALL NEED TO CHANGE . . . SOMETHING . . . MOST THINGS . . . ANYTHING . . . EVERYTHING.

"For the last two weeks, I enjoyed my body just as it was without feeling compelled to change it." I shared this victory with the other four members of my female entrepreneur support group, my informal board. One member of our group had suggested this structure each time we got together. We would share 1) any successes, 2) where we needed support, and 3) an optional wild card update. Each person shared beautifully on all their successes that were piling up. I was thinking ahead about what I might share. I hadn't even noticed ENOUGH tiptoe into the room to take a seat in the circle. My heart kept expanding, as I listened to each successive woman claim her victory—big and small. When my turn came, I was surprised by the first success that slipped past my logical brain and right out of my mouth before I noticed: "For the last two weeks, I enjoyed my body just as it is without feeling compelled to change it." Fourteen entire days, I had stepped into an alternate reality where, for a quick breath of a moment, I didn't feel the need to change something (my body), which had been, by far, the most significant change project of my life since age five.

Let me be clear. I always reserve the right to change anything about my body, from how or what I eat to the way I move any time I want. I also reserve the right to hate my body and rage at it at any unforeseen time. But at that moment, it struck me that I hadn't spent time and energy trying to change anything, and it had freed up space for me to do some other things, so I bragged about it. I increased productivity and creativity in other areas of my life by conserving energy in this area. ENOUGH plopped herself right on my lap as I explained my brag.

In this sweet, small, powerful claim, I discovered that choosing not to change is a completely valid choice. Maybe that's obvious to you. But firecrackers in my brain! I could really enjoy not improving myself? For real?!!

I spent much of my life as a seeker. I took and led personal and professional development courses, devoured books, talks, audios, hired coaches, and attended trainings. I love the way new experiences invite possibilities and alternatives. You see something from someone else's viewpoint, and you realize an entirely new path opens to you. So yes, my bookshelf features a wide variety of invitations (books) to new spaces. At the same time, I was learning that NOT ENOUGH finds a foothold in these spaces more than I would like to admit.

At its highest, personal development invites us to unleash the dormant dreams in our hearts. But personal development can become another ladder we step up on. Without noticing it, we may begin to define the correct way of becoming a better person, a more conscious person, or a more loving person. Bam! Once again, we have created a ladder we can use as a measuring stick (guilty as charged). I may be bad at X, but when it comes to being a good "growthful" person, I'm absolutely better than *them* (said as I glance down my nose and down the ladder).

Personal development challenges us to change. But do we need to? Who made that rule anyway? What's wrong with me, just as I am, with all my humanity and imperfections? Look at our ads and products. Don't they constantly invite us to change something about ourselves? Look younger. Get a faster car. Lose weight. Become a meditator. Make millions. Upgrade the house. Get another house. Be healthy (according to the specific definition of the season). Wear skin-tight pants. Wear wide-leg pants. Be more conscious. Smoke to look cool. Don't smoke to be cool. Get the latest gadget. I mean *this* next gadget. That old thing? That's outdated. How about this next gadget? Are you volunteering enough or changing humanity enough?

Change can be wonderful if . . . if we want it . . . if it brings us joy . . . if it allows us to increasingly enjoy the journey of life we have chosen. But change can be poison masquerading as candy. If I force myself to change to fit in or align with someone else's expectations, then I discard my freedom, my agency, and my choice.

Choice

I think that ENOUGH likes to hang out with Choice. I picture them holding hands, skipping down the path together. I see them as young girls playing side by side the most fantastic game of make-believe. When I remember I have a choice, the world of possibilities expands. I can choose to make more money or less money. I can choose to cook or not cook. I can choose to be wonderfully empathetic or pissed off. Something about claiming these choices and my own agency increases my experience of ENOUGH.

So, of course, I _can_ make many choices, but I don't want to turn those choices into goals I _have to_ achieve. I want them to be possibilities I'm allowed to explore. If I make them goals, I'm right back on that damn ladder.

I met an accomplished physician and senior healthcare CEO who speaks four languages, is an athlete, and has four children. In case your unconscious bias kicked in, she's a woman. Suppose I step on the comparison ladder and consider my ranking vis-à-vis her experience in life (this may or may not have happened in real life, no comment). Hypothetically, if I were getting on the ladder of comparison with her, I have either already lost so badly (not anywhere near her spot on the ladder) that I have given up, or I need to expend a great deal of energy to matter and move into her zip code on the ladder.

But what if I don't have to choose either of these options? What if I step off the ladder and let her continue to enjoy what appears to be a magnificent life (although in actuality, I really do not know this as a fact)? I could let her have her skills and history, and I could have my own. I do not have to change just because I think she is better. I don't have to improve anything at all. I can just learn to enjoy the adventure of life that I am creating.

Increasing Acceptance

Embracing choice and making a choice not to change means I increasingly build my muscle of acceptance. My belly may bulge until the end of my days. I don't know. Can I practice increasing acceptance of that reality? If I don't, I run a very big risk of missing or hating a good deal of my life. My belly didn't bulge in my youth, and in this season of life, I experience a lack of bulge about every four to seven years when I choose a particular health or exercise kick. But when I add up all the days and years, if I tie my life enjoyment to that flat belly, I miss a whole lot of life. I have more stress and anxiety, and I avoid a lot of wonderful experiences.

On the other hand, I may feel like doing a bunch of sit-ups. I may feel like lifting weights. I may feel like wandering around the block or walking five miles. I am beginning to wonder what it is like to increasingly accept my belly while reserving the right to change it at any point in time. To me, that is a real choice, real freedom, real agency.

Wanders, Not Walks

Holy crap! Leggings rolled up, shoes in hand. I stood in the shallow, cold October water in Lake Michigan, letting a light breeze brush my face while I looked at a gorgeous expanse of cold water. I felt the sand ridges beneath my feet as I walked back and forth through the shallows. It was a big deal for me, but let me back up and share why.

Danger lurks in measurement for me. I may decide to get out, enjoy the day, and move my body, but in a whiplash slap, I find myself measuring myself. How far did I go? How fast? How long have I been out? How does this compare to yesterday? What does my activity tracker look like for the week? Seemingly harmless questions become NOT ENOUGH beating on his shiny new drums. I get compulsive. I don't *want* to look every five or ten minutes, but my phone drags my eyes to the health icon updates like a kid to candy, robbing the moment of all the exploratory joy and wonder. I tried to stop but massively failed. When I went for a walk, it became a measurement for change. I felt compelled to drive myself to change, and these steps were the measuring ticks on the ruler. I couldn't win, so I decided to stop playing.

Visiting my new friend ENOUGH in her world, in the land of choice and possibilities, I modified a word I use, "walk," in order to better fit my new mindset. I decided I don't go for walks anymore because walks are like runs, a form of exercise one should do to chase some ever-moving endzone with change as the engine. So, I don't go for a walk. I go for a *wander* instead. I may call a friend or two when I'm out on a wander. Sometimes, I get their voicemail and just let them know how I'm doing while I wander. When I wander, I look around. I feel my feet in my tennis shoes and how they feel on the ground. I actually breathe. I notice things. I exist. I live.

So, what happened to land me in Lake Michigan's cooling waters? On a late afternoon wander, I found myself walking along the path by the lake, a short three-quarters of a mile from my home. With the sun shining, I had a strong desire to kick off my shoes and feel my feet in the sand. But I didn't. I found myself walking past the beach. Thankfully, a crack of openness forced me to stop and ask why I was getting in my steps instead of sinking my feet in the sand. I chose a wander that day, but unbeknownst to me, NOT ENOUGH had passed the whisper-mini-megaphone to the part of my brain that loves to track in order to "fix" my body. (NOT ENOUGH uses this tool when he wants to quietly sneak a thought in my brain that appears in a whisper but is really a shout . . . sneaky, that one.)

So, this part of my brain had noticed that if I stopped and went to the sand, I wouldn't get in the same number of steps. I'd take, G-d forbid, fewer steps while putting my feet in the sand. Can you imagine such an outrageous, irresponsible choice?! Luckily, ENOUGH was still gently leading me by the hand, and I was beginning to wise up. I noticed that I was driving change vs. savoring my feet in the sand. After a few timely expletives that underlined my insight, I stopped, unlaced my shoes, and plunged my feet into the sand. Damn! It felt amazing. I started with just sand, but the water beckoned. I made my way toward the baby shallow ripples, pulled up the pants of my leggings, and plunged my bare feet straight in. Cold and refreshing and mind-blowingly joyful, bitch-slapped straight in the heart with a full explosion of delight, that three minutes made a lasting difference.

I still get sparkly and tingly inside thinking about that bad-ass choice. I chose to reframe my walks into wanders. I chose to ignore the familiar well-trod path, and my choice paid off.

Choosing Both (or some of it, or all of it, or none of it)

Have you ever noticed how much change can masquerade as an either/or? Good and bad, right and wrong, up and down? The day I stuck my feet in the water, I ended up walking more than I normally do. I didn't have to. That wasn't the plan. But it happened. Yet, when I first faced the opportunity of the sand, NOT ENOUGH tricked me, striking fear in my heart. He said, "If you stop and savor this windswept moment (insert a particularly sarcastic tone on the windswept word), you will not get in your steps. If you don't get in your steps, you'll be fat forever. Do you want to be fat forever???!!!"

Complete BS, after all. With ENOUGH's encouragement, I savored the experience *and* still got in steps.

NOT ENOUGH seeks quick-fix solutions to gain purchase in my brain: that person is good *or* bad. The choice I made was the right one *or* the wrong one. I either accept myself how I am, *or* I change myself. But my experiences don't bear out this binary way of looking at the world. Deep inside, I long to keep exploring possibilities and accepting myself. Maybe I'll write a song. Maybe I'll learn three more languages. Maybe I'll become an amazing cook. I love the online video of a granny dancing to hip-hop. Maybe I'll dance like they do, and . . . I don't need to. I can nap instead of move, go toward ease over challenge, and love my body while shifting its shape. The more I zoom in on the map of this territory of apparent contradictions, the more I find myself longing for new neural pathways. The pathways that say: *They are not a bad person, but they made really asshole moves and harmed me. I love my thighs, and I choose to tighten them anyway. I can make a shit ton of money, live a life of ease, and treat people really well.*

Choice Expands the Playground

My daughter played a video game where you create your own world as you play. In the game, she had some defined parameters, like the fence around a playground, but within those parameters, she could still do lots of things. The more she'd explore, the more she'd get access to explore, and so on. I think about how we all live in this expanding playground of experience. When I pop on the ladder of comparison, I actually narrow my playground. Climbing the ladder is a completely legit choice. But, for me, the energy and resources I spend climbing can distract me from creating a new land, exploring a different land, going back to a previous land to make some modifications, or sharing my land with someone new.

Choice fuels the game. I get to choose a lot. Shit happens, for sure. I don't always like what comes, but I don't need to add to my challenges by thinking there is one way to do any damn thing.

I am learning that ENOUGH cradles Choice tenderly in her arms as her cherished bestie. Some choices may be forced in our lives based on circumstances. Some choices we have clearly made. But I continue to find that more possibilities exist than I ever realized. Someone tells us how it is supposed to go, and we orient to that. ENOUGH shares her BFF, Choice, with us. Want to change something? Do it. Want to stay the same. By all means, enjoy it!

Lobster Roll and a Beer

I coached a woman executive who had just successfully completed her first big paid speaking engagement. At the airport, getting ready to board the plane back home, she ordered a lobster roll and a beer. She shared this fact with me as if I were a priest behind a confessional screen. On her ladder of comparison, the good or healthy people don't eat lobster rolls and drink beer. She geared herself up for our call to come clean about her error. I think I may have thrown her off with my response, "Did you enjoy it?" She stumbled a bit, trying to make sure she heard the question correctly, so I repeated it. "Did you enjoy it?" "Yes," she finally acknowledged. "Did you regret it afterward or feel like shit? "No," she clearly stated. "Then what's the problem exactly?" She laughed. (I saw ENOUGH hug her from behind, but I held myself back from mentioning it.)

Her real problem? On her ladder of good and healthy, moving up meant changing everything. Change meant exchanging the beer and lobster roll for water and a salad. Moving down meant drinking the beer and eating the lobster roll. I let her know that I would completely support her choice to have something else to eat if she wanted. But she didn't want to. She wanted to eat the lobster roll and drink the beer. She was simply trying to release the shame that came along with it. Too often, we bring shame along with us to the imperative-to-change party. Luckily,

ENOUGH sprays shame-repellant with every footfall. When ENOUGH travels with me, I find it difficult to feel shame no matter what I've done. With ENOUGH, change is always an option but never an imperative.

———

remember:

You don't need to change . . . EVER.

chapter 4

BODY: NOT ENOUGH

YOU NEED TO LOSE WEIGHT. AND GET BETTER CLOTHES. AND SUCK IN YOUR BELLY. AND FLATTER YOUR CURVES. AND PLUCK YOUR EYEBROWS. AND PUT ON LIPSTICK. AND WEAR THOSE HEELS. AND STRAIGHTEN YOUR HAIR. AND . . .

I noticed my normal panic creeping up—that two-headed snake that starts running from my heart and gut simultaneously to intertwine into a full-grown swirl of shame that only accompanies these horrifying events. The occasion? A wedding of two good friends.

Maybe you love weddings and can't wait to go, but if you are a human who has struggled with your weight or body image or has my superpower of shapeshifting (I can regularly expand between a size 6 and 16 without blinking an eye) you may understand where I am coming from. If you have owned clothing in many sizes, have desperately rubbed self-tanner or lotion into pale jiggly skin, or have squeezed yourself into the latest version of shapewear—you know the terror I'm talking about.

A wedding should be a delightful occasion to enjoy the company of friends and celebrate people you care about. But if you haven't yet jumped on the self-love body positivity train, a wedding can morph into sheer and utter hell. And even if you are thin enough, pretty enough, and settled enough to avoid the gymnastics I do, I would be shocked to discover that you don't keep your own checklist from NOT ENOUGH as the event approaches.

A New Perspective

For this wedding, though, my muscle of ENOUGH had been starting to build a bit. Rather than being disgusted by my extra weight, I had a slightly different experience.

I was getting ready for the rehearsal dinner, I initially panicked. Standing in the stark bathroom hotel light, staring at my unpainted, crackly toenails, I realized I hadn't made time to get the obligatory pre-wedding pedicure. And if that didn't pose a problem, my pants weren't quite fancy enough. The combination of clothes I was sporting didn't quite go together like I had pictured in my mind. I had packed these items because they fit, even though they didn't perfectly coordinate. Normally, these thoughts pulled me down the spiral of shame and embarrassment. Instead, I had the most outrageous thought, hitting me like a Harry Potter lightning strike to the forehead. *Not one person at this event will likely notice or care or remember whether or not my toes are painted.* Why? Because they will be a) too dammed wrapped up in celebrating the brides who are getting married to notice and b) perseverating over all of their own insecurities.

Did I naively think the other guests wouldn't scan for beauty or judge people? No. As a human, I do this all the time. I believe scanning, critiquing, and finding what could be better in myself and others is a completely normal part of the human experience. And if you are the Buddha-elevated person who has risen above such mundane activities, *bless your heart!* But for me, I realized that, at the end of the day, nothing I would do to adjust my external looks would have any significant lasting impact on my life or theirs. Totally. Mind. Blowing.

Now, you may conclude that, with this profound insight, I settled into myself, delighted in the joy of my very being, and reveled in bliss. Completely not true. But - I did save a lot of time and anxiety by *not* perseverating about anything. I finished getting ready and went to the event. My top was beautiful and made me smile . . . ditto for my earrings. My shoes didn't match my outfit at all, and the black pants

I wore under my silk tunic top were really stretch black jeans rolled under. Yet, with a slight squinch of delight, I thought . . . *No one will remember. Ever.* I was right.

To Train or Not to Train

The fertile ground of my body readied for something. What? Some strength, I thought. I talked to a friend who employed a personal trainer. Such a scary word, trainer. Trainers are "other" to me. Trainers like to go to gyms, run, work out, and make other people do these deplorable activities in order to create an acceptable body. At least, that was my not-so-mature definition.

I told my friend, "I am ready, but I have a very specific agenda, so I need to interview this trainer to see if they align with my values." I told her that I want someone who 1) comes to my house, 2) honors, respects, and follows my agenda, 3) cares about strength from the inside out for the long haul (not hyping a person up for a wedding-ready body that shines for a flash until the weather changes), 4) works step by step without pushing and 5) creates a space I look forward to joining once a week, every week for a long time.

She referred him. We talked. I hired him. The first session was amazing. My dear, sweet muscles woke up from a very long winter's nap, and they savored the soreness. How I had missed my muscles, and I didn't even know it! The lovely, easy, achy sensation reminded me I existed without even inviting NOT ENOUGH to comment.

Pure heaven! I was already looking forward to week two. I felt comfortable enough to mention during our session that I had put on 30 pounds over the last couple of years. Little did I know that I had created my own tripwire.

My kind, lovely trainer enthusiastically texted me within the hour. He cheered me on for my great work and got me excited about feeling good. My heart felt expansive as I read the long text paragraph until . . . the other shoe dropped. The text read, "*. . . and by the way, those 30 lb.? I think you could lose them in three months. Or two months. Or even faster. This week, eat x and y and avoid z. You'll see!*"

I imagine many people would delight in this type of enthusiasm or confidence in my ability. Instead, my heart sank through my shoes. To me, the text had propped the door wide open for my old companion, NOT ENOUGH. You see, I had no intention of doing anything about my eating or my extra weight. In the previous months, I had been working diligently on accepting the extra weight and being gentle with myself. My body's openness to considering strength work was a big step—and the *only* step I had chosen to let myself consider at that point.

Under these circumstances, I would normally invite in NOT ENOUGH. I'd offer him coffee and a comfy sofa to rest on and let him live rent-free under my roof for the foreseeable future. In fact, I'd turn up the volume on his chitchat, *"I told you those 30 pounds are a problem. He was hopeful for you, but clearly, you have to do something about all that weight. You better restrict yourself until you look acceptable. In fact, cover yourself in baggy clothes, avoid going out at all costs, and get going on whatever eating plan he suggests. I sure hope you can be successful this time. You know it never lasts, but at least you can look less embarrassing for a while."*

At that point, I would exit my body, numbly nod my head yes, and make some halfhearted commitment to do whatever eating plan my trainer suggested. At some point, though, I would eventually stop following through on that commitment. Rather than tell my trainer I was not succeeding at his suggestions, I would eventually become too busy to do the workout because I could avoid being asked about my eating. I would find a way to end this new workout relationship. And so, with his one simple, innocent text to me, our relationship was over, and my trainer didn't even know it!

But ENOUGH softly offered her encouragement. Her gentle whispers become an electrical current running from my receptive ears to my chest, down my arms, and right to my texting fingertips. I knew there was another way. I breathed. I thought. I stayed in my body instead of exiting it. I sensed its desires and needs. Then I texted back, "Hey, I completely love your appreciation and enthusiasm. But I have no desire to do anything about food or my weight. If I happen to lose weight or size, that is lovely, but I don't want to focus on it at all. I just want to focus on looking forward to this workout every week." His text response came quickly and rapidly with a very apologetic tone, "I'm so sorry. I didn't mean to upset you or step into somewhere I don't belong. No problem. You're doing great. Let's keep going."

Whoa! My heart felt like the Grinch who stole Christmas. It grew two sizes that day. I had allowed ENOUGH to break someone else's unconscious agenda. I had fiercely loved myself in a short text exchange, and the results were amazing. I doubled my commitment to him because he had respected my agenda and my boundaries. I quadrupled my commitment to myself and my vision. I chose ENOUGH for my body, and that choice created elbow room for something that brought me immense joy for quite a while.

How often do we slip down the slide of someone else's agenda (even if they don't know they have one)? How often do we spend our time doing something that feels required, important, necessary, or *right* because we saw it out there? Our commitments desperately need us to re-examine them through the lens of ENOUGH. Does this activity, this person, this agreement support my sense of ENOUGH? My feeling of ENOUGH? The space of ENOUGH? Or did my good intentions slide into an indictment or proof that I'm still NOT ENOUGH? Let me not make it anyone else's job to define my sense of well-being. They don't need that responsibility. They have their own sense of well-being to monitor. In fact, let me do them a big favor by introducing them to my ENOUGH so that their ENOUGH can rise to its highest purpose and meet me. What a gift to them, to me, and to the planet!

Follow Your Body, It Knows the Way

Have you ever noticed that your body guides you impeccably? My body behaves like a finely tuned internal GPS, with a quality rating beyond any German engineering. It never malfunctions. I have owned this engineering marvel for quite some time, and rather than following its impeccable readouts, I have often ignored it. You know what I mean, right? You're in a meeting, and someone says something completely inappropriate. And that comment lands right there, immediately, in your body. Somewhere inside you, a cluster of cells screams (maybe in your gut, maybe in your heart, maybe in your solar plexus), "OMG! Are you kidding? Did you just say that insulting/patronizing/belittling/ignorant comment? In front of all of us???"

But rather than respond to that impeccable instrument of the body GPS, you may shift your focus to your less-than-helpful head, who starts to reason with you. The head brain (IMHO), when not fully integrated with our body, can do a lot of strange reasoning in hilarious and distorted ways. Your head brain may tell you ridiculous things like,

"Well, maybe that *was* an insulting/patronizing/belittling, ignorant comment, but no one else said anything, so it must be okay!" Or "I know that was a hideous, ugly, underbelly slimy statement, but you don't want to embarrass yourself by saying something to your boss, do you?"

I lived this way all of the time. Let's say I went to the store to buy something, and the salesperson had the best clothes and the perfect sales pitch, and yet, the entire time they were talking, tiny little gnawing monsters nibbled at my internal organs, saying, "Stop. Set down your credit card and walk away." A lot of times, I didn't. I couldn't find any logic in my head about why this person wasn't the right one to buy from, or why the product wasn't right for me, or why the timing felt off, so I'd complete the transaction only to regret it later.

What I continue to discover is that my body always communicates with me, guiding me to choices that are aligned and leading me away from choices that are not. My body guards my best interests when I remember that it is not an inconvenient skin sack but a finely tuned instrument.

My Internal GPS: A Finely Tuned Instrument

I worked for a while in clothing stores, and my body warning system would impeccably alert me to shoplifters. I didn't think much of it at the time, but looking back, the instances showed the perfection of this wonderful physical instrument. I stood in the back of a women's boutique where I worked, and I saw a person approach the mall entrance of the store. I immediately told the assistant manager that she needed to approach this person because the woman was about to steal a dress.

The manager looked at me sideways, but maybe because of my very direct tone, she walked over to greet the supposed shopper. Although the woman didn't have time to steal a dress, the manager saw that the woman was trying to tuck a dress under her shirt, which clearly held the bulge of items from another store. Needless to say, the potential shoplifter released the items and walked right out.

Another time, I worked in a home goods department. A very polished, successful suburban businessman came to our counter to return some drapery panels. I stood at the counter and began the transaction, but my belly kept somersaulting. He had no receipt, but technically, he didn't need one.

My logical head brain, which at the time did not have strong linkages to my heart brain, belly brain, or body brain, said, "You silly girl. He is clearly an important man of business. He wouldn't steal from this store. He looks wealthy!" Luckily, I paid attention to my body. I walked to the backroom and told my manager, who, *thank you, Lord,* trusted my instinct.

With glee, my manager said, "Come with me!" I followed him to the back room with the wall of security cameras while he motioned for me to take a seat next to him. "Let's watch," he said with a glimmer in his eye. We watched the man of business stand there for a bit. Then we watched as he began to shift his weight between his two feet. We continued to watch as the man started to glance anxiously around. When I had been away from the sales counter for about five minutes, the man took off jogging toward the exit, leaving all of the merchandise on the counter. YES! Once again, the body GPS won the day! And trust me, I have plenty of other examples. Unfortunately, I can also share an equal number of examples when I ignored my body and paid the price physically or emotionally.

What does following your body have to do with ENOUGH? In my non-scientific opinion, we *all* have this impeccably designed instrument leading us straight to goodness and joy. When tuned in, I can live a life filled with satisfaction, and where my friend ENOUGH regularly frolics in my company, while also leading me away from the things that don't work for me. I believe G-d designed every one of us with this amazing equipment, but NOT ENOUGH yells so loudly we ignore our GPS signaling a new pathway.

Many of us think, *how could I possibly know? If all of society, my friends, my colleagues, and the businesspeople do X and I feel like Y, who am I to question their good sense?* I'll tell you who you are. You are You. You are sufficient just as you are, and your body sensor is leading you to that warm, joyful place of meaningful existence that is yours and yours alone. Your birthright.

ENOUGH reminds me not to design a body to please others. She shows me the wild possibility of creating a body for my own pleasure, a body that tells me when I'm on track and off track. My body still does this even when I am fat or numb or skinny or old or out of touch. Being really brave means tuning in. And if you haven't learned to tune in to yours yet, that is okay too. I'm still learning as well.

My job and your job are not to follow what others think is right or good or best. I believe our existence invites us to increasingly get to know our friend, ENOUGH. When we do, we find miracles. Maybe those miracles lead you to a weekly workout you love. Maybe those miracles lead you to stop a shoplifter. Maybe you'll even enjoy yourself at a wedding or event. And maybe, just maybe, you'll write a song, create some art, start a business everyone else thinks will fail, or even write a book.

Dressing for Me

"Wow, you look nice" (my husband). "Thank you, you sound surprised" (me). "No, it's just I thought you were going to help a friend clean out her house" (my husband). "I am, but these days I'm dressing for me" (me).

Dressing for me? Wham! The words popped out and smacked me on the forehead before I knew what they meant. Sometimes, a big shift happens, but we don't notice it until later. Somewhere, in that month, I had started dressing for myself.

On that Sunday afternoon, I had not dressed up. But I had on white wide-leg jeans and a navy-blue linen shirt. Normally, on my way to help a friend clean out their house, I'd wear my least favorite leggings and a T-shirt. I have no issue with this, by the way, but I got ready that morning and wanted to feel more attractive . . . for me! Sometime long ago, I had let go of the pleasure of dressing. Putting on clothes represented a charade to try and compete in a race I hadn't signed up for. This race guaranteed me a finishing time in the middle of the pack, as I dared not attempt being the best runner, and certainly wasn't going for being the last runner that everyone felt sorry while they shuffle across the finish line. In fact, without noticing it, my life's work in this area had become making sure I didn't fall to the back of the pack. Like the gazelle running from the lioness, I didn't want to be eaten. Sure, I longed to be #1 in that race, but I knew I didn't have the raw resources to do it. Somewhere along the way, I had completely geared my efforts to scanning my audience and making sure I fell in the middle of the pack.

I don't really care if someone chooses to dress well or not, to be fashionable or not. And I love humans who love me just as I am and accept me, dare I say, even enjoy me, no matter what I look like. But in the autopilot choice of my ongoing middle of the pack race, I had left behind some childlike joy of putting together outfits that feel good.

My baby book reads, "loves to dress up and refuses to wear pants." I don't even know that human. Whoever she was massively rebelled as a tree-climbing, mud-playing tomboy tween intentionally wearing a baseball hat and T-shirts as a statement of some youth-filled feminist rebellion. But I left something behind when I did that: the one who wanted to play and make stuff and do crafts and dream stuff up. That four-year-old dress-up gal had a constant companion in ENOUGH. She didn't know a ladder of comparison existed. She made crafts, sang songs, and put on shows for the family at holidays. ENOUGH sat by her side as they dreamed up ideas and worlds and imagined being a gymnast, a skater, or an actress. And somewhere, in growing up, I had left her far, far behind. I find the memory dusty even now. And I feel sad to admit that she didn't leave 10 years ago. She left somewhere around age five.

I distinctly remember being age five and standing on a beach for a photo with my red-checked bikini on. I was highly aware of Kim, the slightly older but much taller, skinny, tan, blond standing next to me in her powder blue bikini. I felt ashamed. Shame at age five. How does this happen? I know how it happens, but that's probably a story for a different book. Suffice it to say that at the age of five,

NOT ENOUGH parked himself in the lens of that camera on the beach at Lake Erie and made sure I knew my place. Without looking, I knew the diameter of her thighs vs. my thighs. Roaming around the campground I watched boys' eyes sparkle as they talked to her and ignored me. I was too young for any of those things to matter at all. But they did. I left my dress-up, creative, have-fun girl on the beach that day.

So, when I proclaimed, "I'm dressing for myself," I wanted to cry. Some part of me had reawakened. The girl who put clothing on her body—not for someone else—but because she enjoyed them. I was reconnected with that girl who wore clothes because she liked how they looked, and because she liked how the colors went together. Like that four-year-old girl, I could wear a dress to play in the mud in the backyard. In fact, that little girl would consider any other choice unthinkable. So, the white pants and blue linen shirt were my modern-day dress . . . impractical maybe, but beautiful to look at, yes, very much. The lens of the camera discarded for the mirror of enjoyment. A critiquing gaze exchanged for a playground.

I would love to tell you I always dress for myself now. I do not. I am learning, with ENOUGH's help, to notice when the four-year-old exits the room and the five-year-old enters. At first, I strategized to avoid situations that would invite the five-year-old to enter. If only I avoided superficial people, or superficial situations, or events where no skinny people congregated, then maybe it would be safe enough to allow the four-year-old to attend. However, avoidance did not represent a long-term strategy. Now I am playing with tucking an imaginary walkie-talkie in my handbag with ENOUGH on the other end. I can whisper to her inside myself when I feel like a five-year-old, and she can respond back with a funny joke, silly remark, or a healthy intervention.

For me, heaven doesn't need to be a place after death with angels, clouds, and harps. Heaven could very much be right here right now. Think of the fun to be had when leaning into that four-year-old joy while unapologetically writing a new play, or singing a new song, or pulling the dress-up clothes out of the closet!

---

remember:

Love your body, listen to your body, follow your body. You picked it.

CHAPTER 5

BEAUTIFUL BOUNDARIES. ZERO APOLOGIES: ENOUGH

"I appreciate the offer, but I am not interested. Thank you." Woo hoo! I had met a woman at a networking event who offered me a free week of business services. No obligations. No charge. No hidden strings attached. I read her email invitation and responded (outrageously for me) . . . "I appreciate the offer, but I am not interested. Thank you." A small "no." Not a big deal. Nothing outrageous for most people. But somewhere along the path of my life, NOT ENOUGH's persistent chatter convinced me that I had an obligation to take what I was given and appreciate it— whether a complimentary service or an invitation for coffee with someone who drains my energy.

Reveling in the Small "no"s or Drowning in the Small "yes"es

With ENOUGH bunking with me in a semi-permanent arrangement, I began delighting in small "no"s. I stopped giving reasons. I stopped justifying or explaining. I made no apologies. I simply said "no." "I have a free ticket to this fundraiser; would you like to join me?" "No but thank you for inviting me." "Are you going to their birthday party?" "No." "Oh, are you out of town?" "No."

Believe it or not, the small "no"s can challenge us more than the big "NO"s. The big "NO" reflexively meets its challenger on the field. Someone does something against our values or affronts our sense of justice, and the big "NO" draws fire from our belly to rise to the occasion. With that clarity, people rarely question us.

On the other hand, the small "no" often elicits indignance or outrage from others. "Why not? Do you have a conflict?" someone might react to my crystal clear "no" response. Oftentimes, NOT ENOUGH lies in wait, belly down in the field, for just this moment. He will pop his head up out of the grass and poke me in the back to respond. I'd startle and then scramble to come up with some acceptable justification, even a lie. Before I know it, the excuse, the phrase, the words leap out of my mouth and into the air, no longer retrievable. I sink a little lower in my shoes. Those experiences are mostly in the past now. With this new empowered stance, I am beginning to delight in the small "no"s. I now wonder how my life was ever in a default mode that demanded I explain my choices.

If we do not learn to honor the small "no"s, we can easily drown in the small "yes"es. "Yes, I'll go to that networking event I don't want to attend." "Yes, I'll drop that off for you." "Yes, I'll store that hideous family tchotchke disguised as an heirloom until you die." "Yes, I'll graciously accept the free book I never intended to read because it came with the cost of my event ticket."

We rationalize that a quick coffee meeting, or the heirloom, will not take up much space after all, but therein lies the rub. A book here, a piece of clothing there, a calendar obligation tucked in over there adds up. This cycle repeats itself over and over again until my home, my calendar, my emotions, and my life no longer offer me a space to rest my weary head. The shelves are filled. The calendar is full. My time is taken . . . and it all happens when I am not paying attention or prioritizing my needs. Before long, I am starring in an episode of *Hoarders*, and I am the one whose metaphoric life and home brims with everybody else's stuff—filled with their desires and requests, not mine.

I have a friend who ran a calendar experiment with herself. She tracked her time to distinguish calendar choices she made for herself vs. others. The results of her research slapped her in the face: a full 95% (!!!) of her calendar reflected someone else's desires, not hers. She was drowning in the small "yes"es.

With small "yes"es we erode our power one teaspoon at a time. On the other hand, when we plant the seed of a small "no," before we realize it, that small seed extends its roots into the ground and raises its hands to the sky, forming a beautiful boundary. The boundary establishes itself when we say no, but the beauty only blossoms when we strip out the apology or explanation.

Releasing the Apology and Explanation

NOT ENOUGH demands that we explain our choice, and ideally, one that matches the ardor of the request. You really, really, really want me to go to the event. I better have a really, really, really good reason for saying no. And to add to the comedy of the farce, social norms require me to preface my excuse with a lie by saying, *I'm sorry:* "I'm sorry.

I would love to go, but I have a really big thing or conflict or fantastic reason I can't make it . . ."

I am absolutely not sorry and should not be sorry when I make a decision that works for me. A sorry in that situation equates to me apologizing for existing. In fact, my honest answer would be, "I'm quite delighted and almost giddy to inform you that I have learned to prioritize my needs so much that I will not be attending. I wish you the same joy I am experiencing as I learn to orient to what matters to me." Don't get me wrong. Sometimes I *am* sorry to miss an event. I may truly want to go and have a prior commitment. If so, I do not hesitate to insert my authentic sorry. The majority of the time, though, I am not sorry for my choices. I am proud of them. I have worked hard to reach a level of clarity that allows me to make these choices without apology, so I am mostly proud, not sorry.

By the way, the askers or givers rarely mean harm in the offering. Generally, the offers contain significant goodwill. For this reason, the only authentic part of the social norm transaction I care to honor is the thank you at the end: "Thank you for inviting me." In my heart of hearts, I am delighted to be invited to anything. When you invite me, I sense that I matter to you in some fashion, and that feels wonderful.

The Big "NO": Letting go of a Person, a Situation, a Path, or a Choice

I am so done! I woke up with a combination of crankiness, raw fatigue, and vulnerability from losing sleep. The previous night, I had tossed and turned as I mulled over a few things that were bugging me. The result was the decision to make a big "NO" to a few things—some ways I had let myself be treated, some personal choices I had made, and some peoples' behavior that I had tolerated far too long.

That morning, after being done, my brain and stomach felt settled, clear, and committed in a new way. I had been spending energy supporting a friend of a friend who did not give back in return.

This woman was kind, friendly, gracious . . . and completely unavailable. I couldn't get in. She was perfect and prepared and organized . . . and I didn't matter to her at all. I could feel it in the river of my DNA. I had become an object to her, a means to an end. She never said that. No one watching us talk would have any clue that was happening. We were both savvy to life's niceties so our verbal volleying looked lovely. But I felt it.

I am not a transactional human. I don't give in exchange for receiving. My giving usually fills up my tank. But that wasn't happening this time, and I noticed. I don't normally notice, but I noticed.

To be completely transparent, I am not a transactional human now, but I have been a transactional human in the past. I have used people. Often. I am definitely no saint when it comes to past relationships, and I probably have thousands of *I'm sorrys* to share before I reckon with my maker. But most of those transactions happened in another season of my life.

In exploring my own becoming, I was increasingly tuning my GPS to authentic mutuality and shared contribution. I love the feeling I have when I talk with someone, share, unfurl, unfold, and allow, and we both walk away feeling expanded and uplifted.

That was not happening at all in this situation with the friend of a friend.

So, I woke up with *I am so done*! The overwhelming sense of my own well-being was a wave crashing over my inhibitions to make a different choice. It didn't matter what she thought. It didn't matter if she didn't understand. It didn't matter if everyone I knew did not understand. I felt it and I . . . was . . . done. It was a big "NO" to this relationship. The path was clear. I'd let her know what was happening. I'd tell her it wasn't a fit. I'd leave the crack in the door open for something more real to peek its hungry head into our relationship, but I wouldn't try to force it.

I originally thought ENOUGH's philosophy meant settling for certain people, situations, or reasonable outcomes. *Be happy with what you have. Don't expect too much. Be grateful.* That was how I described ENOUGH before I met and got to know her.

I no longer believe any of those statements are true.

I think I, you, and everyone we are in contact with came to this world with many possible life paths to explore. I think free will means that we get to feel ourselves, try stuff out, and learn what moves us, uplifts us, and serves us. Free will also means learning what drains us, pulls us down, and rips out our hearts. I think these possible life paths change continuously with every single decision we make.

And all along, ENOUGH constantly talks to us, affirming our right to explore any path we damn well feel like. She also shouts and screams from the top of her lungs, sometimes early in the morning or late at night: "You are ENOUGH! You have ENOUGH! You don't need their approval, or his pat on the head, or her endorsement of your strategy."

ENOUGH never asks us to sit quietly on the sidelines tolerating everything that comes our way. ENOUGH calls to us from the middle of the river, yelling, "Wade in! The water's NOT warm, but you'll feel completely alive!"

I made the move and withdrew my lifeforce from the relationship. I did not cut the person from my life (although I reserve the right to do that at any time), but I stopped overgiving, overserving, and spending my time with her in ways that did not benefit me. I backed out of the parking space to head out on a new adventure, leaving her to her own devices. Months have turned into over a year in that big "NO," and I have never looked back.

A big "NO" doesn't need to look loud or obvious. The big "NO" happens on the inside, and we get to choose how that shows up on the outside. I have surprised myself more often than not in this regard. When I have gotten a clear, big "NO" on the inside, I tend to feel more at ease and at peace which leads to me being more gracious on the outside. Remembering that others' opinions are not my business, I quickly reset my GPS and I'm off!

Layers of Big "NO"s

That morning when I first uttered, "I am so done!" I actually questioned myself briefly. I had uttered, "I am done!" in the past about various situations, people, or circumstances.

I had to ask myself, was I *really* done then? Am I *really* done now?

Here's what I figured out quickly. I was done then, and I am done now. And I reserve the right to be done one thousand more times in the future.

Every declaration of done, every big "NO," formed a ring of the tree that is my life. I created a ring of the tree the first time I said "done." Then, I grew and developed. My roots went deeper. I created another ring the next time

I said done. My branches reached higher and broader. These rings continued to form, season after season. I never go back to being who I was, but those parts of me continue to live inside me as the next level of growth enfolds the previous one.

Beautiful Boundaries: The Energy Equation

The more beautiful boundaries I have established with small "no"s and big "NO"s, the more my vision of possibilities expands. The small "no" of turning down an invitation may have planted a seed and the big "NO" of releasing a relationship may have created more structure to my insides, but the beauty of these boundaries was always changing and delighting me.

I realized a beautiful boundary did not just include my calendar, my stuff, or even my relationships. A beautiful boundary included my energy. Beautiful boundaries reflect obvious choices and subtle choices. Sometimes, I would stand next to someone who kept complaining about the same thing over and over again. Whoosh! I could feel the vacuum of their drama begin to suck my energy. In NOT ENOUGH's reign, I behaved appropriately, always the good citizen, nodding and smiling and piping in little affirming words to support the repeated rant. But these days, NOT

ENOUGH kept slipping off his throne. I saw him bounce his ass on the floor of the court a few times.

These days he was looking like a drunk-ass clown supported by his court jesters. What did I ever see in him anyway? I could have sworn those jesters previously wore well-tailored business suits and looked quite impressive. But that memory was nowhere to be found. They all looked ridiculous. I might still find myself standing next to an energy vacuum, but ENOUGH would catch my eye from across the room and point out the beautiful garden with spring blossoms outside. I'd excuse myself and go for a short walk in nature, allowing my energy to refill, replenish, and nourish me in many ways.

The energy restoration and battery recharge also required me to notice whom I physically allowed in my spaces. My entire measuring stick changed. My compulsion to compare and measure myself against others has not yet disappeared, but more measuring instruments made their way into my bag. I began to ask myself questions such as: "Does my heart feel expanded and open when I am with this person?" And: "Do I feel better about myself after they leave?" If so, my battery usually filled up more. For others, my battery neither drained nor charged. And still others, like my complainer, drained me fully and sucked the life force straight from me with a surprising vigor. ENOUGH led me to explore new possibilities of how I spent my time, where I spent my time, and with whom I spent my time.

Beautiful boundaries hadn't restricted me to smaller spaces. These boundaries were creating new pathways that led to entirely new vistas.

Research proves this BTW. When you create a playground with no fence or boundary, children play tightly together in the middle to create safety. On the other hand, when you create a boundary, or put a fence around even a large space, the children will expand their play to reach all of the spaces. Without beautiful boundaries, I had not felt safe. I had played in a tight, small circle with the same people in my life. As ENOUGH taught me the power of beautiful boundaries, more life became available. I was the child who couldn't wait to explore every bit of this beautiful existence.

———

remember:

Create beautiful boundaries with zero apologies.

CHAPTER 6

MONEY: NOT ENOUGH

WE DON'T HAVE ENOUGH MONEY FOR THAT. OR FOR THIS. FOR TRAVEL OR FOR BUYING OR FOR BUILDING OR FOR . . . ONCE WE HAVE "IT" THEN WE'LL . . . ONCE I MAKE ENOUGH, THEN I'LL . . . ONCE I RETIRE, THEN I'LL . . .

Does anyone ever have enough money? What is that anyway? Appetites grow with pocketbooks. Comparisons grow with wealthy friends. I thought when I arrived here, at this place in my life, that this would be enough. Spouse. Children. Lovely home. Good neighborhood. Friends. Job. What happened? Who pushed the endzone while I ran down the field? It's like walking down a hallway that never ends, or dreams where you are just about to make it to the oasis, only to find out the oasis is a mirage.

If you look closely enough, the cracks in the veneer present themselves. That really perfect couple over there? She's having an affair. That multi-millionaire over there? He is suicidal. That beautiful social media influencer? Their company is falling apart, but no one knows. Shhhhh. Don't say that I told you.

Let me be clear. You and I need money to put food on the table and clothes on our backs. If you have those basic things mostly covered, you are more privileged than most of the planet. For some odd reason, we have not yet created a world where baseline security is a human right. But if you have that baseline, you (and I) have the gift of being able to reflect on the value we give to money. Money doesn't bring more heaven or more hell. Money doesn't care.

Don't get me wrong. I absolutely love money. I welcome it in as a sweet friend. That is my choice. But to pretend that I could follow the money line, hoping to find my friend ENOUGH on the other end? No way in hell.

The Abundant Little Patch

The patch of dirt that was supposed to be a garden in front of our house looked bad. From my perspective then, we didn't have enough money to do something different.

Someday maybe we'd invest in . . . bushes and shrubs, maybe a landscaper, maybe just a design, or something to do. I looked at the front garden patch, fantasizing about its future when the money came in . . . that magical fantasy time when I'd unveil my mental plan for a social-media-worthy lawn design of gorgeousness. I stared at the bare patches of earth between the plants with my hungry fantasies.

I love that I can envision beautiful things. I'm actually pretty good at it. Quite often, my visions come true. But this was something different: a massive focus on NOT ENOUGH standing in my front yard, legs spread and arms crossed.

As ENOUGH continued to live with me, something shifted. I planted one thing in that empty front patch, a random little plant friend, and I watched her because she was mine. I loved her from afar and wished her to grow because I had birthed her there . . . completely imperfect, exactly where she was. And I felt joy at knowing I had helped. I had made a difference in that one small way in the otherwise ugly patch. A strange thought struck me. I felt the urge to bring in another little plant being, so I did. And another. And another. None of these plant beings found themselves inscribed on a master plan. None of them cost much money. But, plant by plant, over the long haul, I ran into a new problem. The front patch became so full, that I had a hard time seeing any open spaces left to bring in any new leafy friends.

One day, I was walking down our street, and I met a neighbor who lived a couple blocks away. Her yard looks like a wild science experiment, with plants and statues and things scattered everywhere—the house everyone in the neighborhood knew had the bright purple porches. I met that neighbor, and I don't know why, but we immediately connected. We talked about plants. I knew nothing about them. She knew everything about them. She was in her eighties. She looked like she was in her sixties even though she used a wheelchair as a walker to push herself around in the garden. She invited me into her house, which was getting gutted and rehabbed from a fire three years earlier. She told me about her yoga, her Korean roots, and that she loved G-d. She told me that the neighbors across the street were letting her stay with them while her house got reworked on the inside. Her yard was very ugly to some people. She told me this, and she told me she didn't care. She declared unapologetically that she loved whimsy and would say it directly to anyone who had the guts to comment to her face. She had made friends with so many things that had roots.

Everywhere you looked, something was thriving. From a garden tour through her eyes, not my own or anyone else's, I could see the perfect rightness in the abundance of this lawn or garden or experience. I told her about my ugly patch that had now become a lovely patch.

She told me to come back the next morning, and she would share some of her root friends with me. I felt

ENOUGH very much at work in this relationship, so I woke up early, grabbed my son to come along, and loaded up my wagon with some wild geranium from my yard to share with her. Ironically, I had never planted the wild geranium in my yard to begin with. The seeds had blown over from a neighbor's yard, and they had decided to grow abundantly where they landed. I just let them go and now I had plenty to share.

My son and I pulled our geranium-filled wagon down the block to see our neighbor. Sure enough, she was out front, tending and watering and growing and welcoming us. She made direct eye contact with my teenager when she talked to him, and he responded in kind. She proceeded to walk around her garden yard and tug at some plants while describing what they were and what they liked. She kept loading our arms and the wagon until nothing else would fit. I watched her pull up one of her root friends and I had the oddest, most beautiful, physical sensation. The plant looked to me like a long-shaped human being with its roots dangling like legs from her hand. I felt as though she was sharing her very real friends with me.

When we thought the wagon could not hold anymore, we hauled our new friends home and immediately planted them. I felt like these friends had willingly come with me and were now moving to my house. This exchange, this sharing, this love fest of plant life, woke something in me. I watered. I tended. I cared. I watered. I tended. I cared.

A very surprising thing happened shortly after. A neighbor couple walked by. They said they loved my front patch and that they regularly walked by and admired it. It really made them happy. I was shocked. Did this couple just rave about my formerly ugly patch? Even though I could not find the bare patches to plant, I still thought of this front area as my unfinished yard. I looked with new eyes at the former ugly patch. The area really was quite beautiful. Not perfect. Beautifully imperfect and abundant. Somewhere along the way I had stopped focusing on the ugly.

I had planted new life, and I had given my attention to that new life. I had given my attention to what I did have, not to what I did not have. My attention had begun to notice the beauty and the diversity and how much there was. I realized that for this particular patch of land, I no longer needed any money. I didn't need a plan. I didn't need a design. Were there things I wanted to shift or improve? Absolutely. But I knew ENOUGH. I also had a new contact down the block—a neighbor who possessed a treasure box of plant life in her yard. If I ever felt like filling an empty patch, I could simply walk down the block with my wagon and load it up.

I feel like plants and fruits and seeds celebrate ENOUGH in songs and sways. They grow tall and fat, bushy and poky, large and small. They make new babies . . . on their own . . . all the time. They give and give and give while asking nothing in return. They remove toxins from our air and, if tended to, make more beauty for us. They can't seem to help themselves. Even when conditions aren't quite right, they try to grow and spread. Sometimes things get in their way, but they keep sharing themselves anyway. They are not soft in their ENOUGHness. They are fierce and determined. They break through concrete if necessary to assert their life force. We don't notice. We pass by them, blind to their lessons. But they don't need us to affirm their worship of ENOUGH. They just are. They give us even more in the face of our indifference.

Money, ENOUGH, and Business

Don't help them. If you do, they'll take your business. They are your business competitor. If they are successful, there will be less room for you. You can nod, be nice, and smile, but don't let them in on your plan. What if they do better at your plan than you do? They probably will.

I got an automated link from an online community that asked me for a recommendation for a woman who was doing exactly what I was doing for my emerging business. My original gut reaction? Defensive. Protective. *How can I recommend her? Dare I? I like her. I met her. She's great. I'd hire her. But . . . she does what I do. What if I recommend her and people do business with her instead of with me? How can I recommend someone else for the things I do? If she takes all that business, what will I have?* These were definitely NOT ENOUGH's social media posts running through my mind.

But even science contradicted NOT ENOUGH's vehement push. Science tells us that the universe keeps expanding. If the universe is the pie, then the pie keeps expanding. How can each of us decide whether or not there is enough to go around when it keeps growing? It's really silly when you think about it, but it's really sobering when you consider it.

Writing this book forced an accountability and commitment in my relationship to ENOUGH I hadn't anticipated. I thought about ENOUGH as soon as I received the automated link looking for a recommendation. After a little bit of imaginary internal chitchat back and forth with ENOUGH, I settled into myself. If I recommend this woman and people do business with her, then they do business with her. That business will bring her joy, and she will be filled with even more happiness because I said true things about her, and she got business out of it. This thought felt quite daring. Was I willing to be that generous? After all, I was just starting out, and she had an established, successful business.

"F*ck it!" ENOUGH shouted to me over the noisy tempest of my internal dialogue—unusual as up until this point, she spoke very little. I think she was getting comfortable with our relationship and even getting a little sassy. "Throw caution to the wind!" she shouted. I closed my eyes and thought about what to say about this woman that was the most honest, the most real, and the most compelling. I let it spill out through my fingers. I dared to tell our shared audience how great she was without apology. I scattered my love to the wind in her review.

And then, just as I hit the submit button, I felt her sneak up behind me again. That warm sun radiating from my heart. That joy. That uplifting sensation. That expansion. Oh! My heart caught like a sleeve on a hook. Crying, I thought, *I might or might not get business because of this review, but I already got so much more . . . and immediately.* I felt a warm burst of love injected straight into my system with no intermediary. Isn't this why people try to make a lot of money and build businesses and look fancy? Aren't they looking for the injection of joy I just received at no charge, costing no more than a few minutes of my time?

Priceless Treasures

We sat next to each other on the couch, tears streaming down my face. My friend, who consistently followed a morning ritual of reading a daily meditation, had just been sharing today's message out loud with me. I remember the meditation was about trading judgments and criticisms for observations. The reading struck a deep chord that signaled my waterworks to begin flowing. You see, a battle had been waging in my heart and belly. Over the last month, I had been swinging wildly between judging others for what they had or judging myself for what I didn't. When my friend read the daily reflection, I burst into tears, confessing to her that I felt like an addict to this battle. I knew better in every part of my body, but I couldn't stop.

My friend shared a completely different perspective on my struggle. In her eyes, the entire thing hadn't been a battle at all but an experience I was having as I was learning about myself through my relationship with others. Then it hit me like a ton of bricks. Not only was I not fighting a battle of light and dark within me, but what I really felt happening was NOT ENOUGH kicking and screaming out of rage.

ENOUGH had made a regular home in me, so much so that it had become my new norm. I knew she and I had been building a friendship, but somewhere along the way, she had brought over a toothbrush and filled a drawer with her belongings. She had been preparing to make a more permanent home. NOT ENOUGH knew the implications. Although he'd never be completely banished, a clear tradeoff was happening. The more she took up space, the less space was available to him. This psychic battle was not a crisis to solve; it certainly wasn't anything to panic about. The tears kept coming.

That afternoon I wondered about the value of that conversation. I wondered how one puts a price on the cost of another soul holding witness to your pain and mess and reflecting back only beauty. Suddenly, in the blink of an eye, money had returned to its rightful place in my personal story: an asset to create, a tool that allows me to contribute, a joyful invitation to some earthly pleasures. The kind of abundance that a moment like that holds is hard to describe. Sometimes a friend or confidant creates space for ENOUGH in a relationship. My friend seemed to pat the tiny space on the couch between us and invite ENOUGH to sit down and make her magic.

The whole interaction didn't last more than fifteen minutes before others joined us, but her space-making for ENOUGH had the same effect as my first sidewalk chalk experience. Time stopped and stretched again. I came to the couch as a beggar, and I left as a queen with unlimited riches.

I Still Love Money

Smooch, smooch! I kiss my paychecks when I receive them. I also draw rainbows, hearts, and stars on them. I thank the money coming to me, and I love receiving it. I love to do a little jig when money is automatically deposited into my account after a consulting engagement. I can't say I always oriented to money this way. I have had the blessing of many authors whose work I have had the privilege to consume that has helped me to develop this recent relationship.

In an either/or world, I think it is easy to quickly lose sight of the fact that money neither charts my way to ENOUGH's home nor blocks my path. Money is money. A chair is a chair. A ruler is a ruler. A hammer is a hammer. Once I meet my basic needs, I give money any greater power over me. Sometimes, I have chosen to put money at the head of an authoritarian regime doing the bidding of NOT ENOUGH. I certainly do not have this handled, but I have discovered some truly surprising things as I have shifted my relationship with money.

When I launched my business, I discovered that when I overreacted and freaked out about money (listened to NOT ENOUGH), my pipeline of leads dried up. On the other hand, when I calmed my nerves and went for a walk or reached out to meet people, possibilities emerged. I started describing this dynamic to friends to keep myself in check when I got nervous. (And yes, I still do periodically freak out, and I reserve the right to my humanity in this regard.)

I initially thought I was weaving some wonderful witchcraft with my intent, but I think the answer remains simpler. Money is a tool, just like that hammer. With a hammer, I can build someone a chair or hit myself on the head. The same is true for money. I can build a beautiful business or hit myself over the head out of terror or comparison. The hammer doesn't care how I use it; the same goes for money. So, I get to pick how I interact. I have now chosen money as a beautiful, creative playmate who helps me eat, go to school, buy clothing, write a book, put on a show, take a friend to lunch, travel, or have any other wonderful experience. At the same time, I don't always need money to do those things. Sometimes, someone takes me to lunch, gives me clothes, or offers lodging for a sweet trip.

At the core, we have been duped into building economies that depend on money earning in exchange for existing. Somebody set up that game a long time ago under the guise of making trade easier. But if all our cash burned up and every bank disappeared, I am fully convinced ENOUGH would lead us out to the fields to grow and share our food. She'd bring us together to build housing for all. She'd help us exchange goods and clothing and whatever else we needed. As we practice staying in our energy lane, that beautifully unique area where we can impact change, we should let money do the same. Money doesn't need to save us any more than a hammer.

———————

remember:

Love and enjoy money, but don't ask it to lead you to ENOUGH.

CHAPTER 7

STAY IN YOUR ENERGY LANE: ENOUGH

OMG. DID YOU HEAR WHAT THEY ARE DOING? THEY SHOULD DO THIS. I CAN'T BELIEVE SHE DECIDED TO DO THAT. SHOULD I TELL HER TO DO THAT INSTEAD OF THIS? DO I NEED TO TAKE CARE OF HIM, HER, THEM, THAT?

"You shouldn't put up with that. You should tell him the truth. You aren't a doormat!" I poured on unsolicited advice as if it were my battle, not hers. Mired in a friend's drama, I caught myself while I was thankfully only ankle-deep. I graciously turned down my volume and my vehemence and suggested they do whatever felt right for them. Sometimes,

I lost track of ENOUGH, like a little kid searching for their parent in a grocery store aisle. Instead of getting distracted by candy, I'd get distracted by someone else's problems until I was so immersed I no longer knew where I was. Thankfully, I was learning that living with ENOUGH meant staying in my own energy lane, the corner of the drama that has to do with my decisions, not someone else's. Easier said than done.

Sometimes, I step out of my energy lane to try to feel better about my own pain by solving someone else's problem. Other times, the ladder of comparison leads me out of my energy lane as I try to be better than someone else. Neither of these strategies actually leads to well-being, peace, or success.

My Ray or Yours

ENOUGH showed me a visual one day that really helped educate me on staying in my energy lane.

Imagine that we all start as one unified whole at the center of a glowing star, like the sun. Picture every soul on the planet joined in one composite unit. Now imagine rays that emanate from that unified whole or center, just like the rays of a sun. Imagine that each one of those energy rays is the path for one individual on the planet. To be their most magnificent, they are meant to start at that center and follow that path outward, always expanding. And imagine that if everyone did that, the glow of magnificence would be beyond our comprehension. Imagine that each of us expands that core glow, reaching even more and more dark spaces within the universe to light it up.

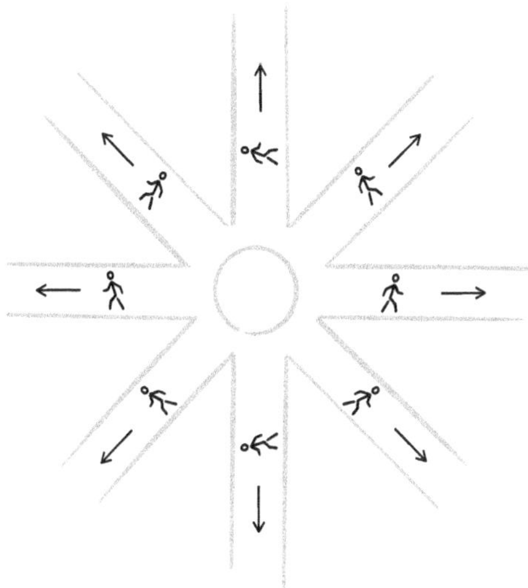

ENOUGH comes to you, gently takes your hand, and leads you toward the energy lane that is perfectly designed for you. As you set foot in that energy lane, you step onto the most amazing moving sidewalk that quickens your pace with little effort and brings you immense joy. Living in your energetic lane brings you tremendous meaning, hope, inspiration, and joy.

All good. Very doable. Simple path. Simple instructions. Full benefits. All you, I, and we need to do is to stay in our lane. And yet we don't. ENOUGH invites us, gently grabbing our hand, but we look to the side, to the ray's path next to us, and we hear the siren song: "Your ray is great but look at this ray. Isn't this ray wonderful? Don't you want to be on this ray?" We hop out of our energy lane and onto that ray, into that energy lane. We briefly startle as we realize that someone else is already standing in that energy lane before us. The siren song we heard was . . . no surprise . . . NOT ENOUGH, hiding behind someone else's bright light to tempt us out of our energy lane and into theirs. But we reason that this new energy ray is great. Maybe NOT ENOUGH talks truth this time, we reason . . . maybe this one is better.

The problem? Someone is always in your way, always in front of you. The person who calls this energy ray home will always be present on the moving sidewalk in front of you. You may want to pass them. You may convince yourself that you can be better at their energy lane than they are. But in the end, you set yourself up for an inevitable failure. They can never and will never let you pass. And they shouldn't. No one can ever be better at being them than they are. And try though you might, you will never succeed.

In the meantime, your energy lane remains empty. ENOUGH patiently waits, periodically calling you back home, but your mind has been poisoned to think that somehow, in some way, this new space is superior to your perfectly fitted, customized light beam.

I have often found myself jumping into someone else's energy lane. I know better, but I still do it. Somewhere along the way, I made up the rules that somehow I am meant to be in someone else's lane, sometimes admiring it, sometimes giving them advice on what to do there.

The source of all sends us out from our home, our center, our connectedness, on our rays to expand and light the dark. If we stay in our lane, we coexist with many beautiful rays, all creating a magnificent glow. But if we hop into someone else's energy lane, we create tension within ourselves. We keep trying to win a game that wasn't designed for us. And our beautiful lane remains a little more dimmed than necessary.

Just Be Yourself

Just be yourself. I figured that if I could just be myself, then I would stay in my energy lane. But that phrase pissed me off. For decades! Being myself felt like another tall order I was supposed to fill, but I didn't even know the basic ingredients. Who the hell is *myself* anyway? Is myself the young girl I was, the painful teens and twenties I navigated, the adult human? Did *be myself* mean doing the things I'm good at? If so, what were they? Did *be myself* mean I needed to go on some quest to discover my calling, my bliss, my joy so that I could follow it? No matter how many ingredients I gathered, I could never put them together to make a tasty dish.

I feel like I am just starting to get the phrase a little bit more. Staying in my energy lane does not mean fulfilling some very large and detailed agenda of being myself that is hidden from me. As ENOUGH began to take up more and more space in my life and my heart, I learned that being myself wasn't a place to land but an experience to have, and being myself often changed. One day, being myself meant I hated yogurt, and a couple of months later, being myself meant loving eating yogurt. Being myself means following the flow of my ever-changing desires, giving myself permission to be in a moment-by-moment discovery. I have always been a seeker of the deeper truths, an explorer of the mysteries, but now staying in my energy lane means I can explore with no real need to find an answer. These days often my biggest challenge is sitting in the discomfort of discovering long enough to feel the joy of it.

Sitting in Discomfort

Having spent so much time trying to hop into many people's energy lanes, I knew not to do that, but what should I do instead? ENOUGH invited me to sit still with my discomfort. As NOT ENOUGH came knocking on my belly door urging me to get out and fight someone else's fight, ENOUGH began training me to sit still and notice but not engage. Sitting still instead of fighting made me uncomfortable. I had trained myself to go to battle with NOT ENOUGH, to contradict and counteract and counterattack, which really just led to me puffing myself up. And once again, I'd be turning my inferiority into false superiority, and climbing back on that ladder.

But one day, ENOUGH shared a very small but very powerful secret. While NOT ENOUGH was knocking loudly, calling me out to the battlefield, ENOUGH leaned over and spoke (this out-loud voice of hers was still new to me, BTW), "When you fight, you give him power." Massive mic drop! All the battling I had been doing, thinking I was getting ahead in this fight to feel okay, was creating the opposite result. NOT ENOUGH loved to fight. He delighted in pressing my buttons and calling me to the open field to duel. He knew that when I got charged or triggered or worked up, my energy increased. When my energy increased, he drank from that fountain. I thought I was doing something purposeful by jumping in that energy flow, but I was simply stepping out of my energy lane and feeding my enemy. I'd leave the battles proud that I was a strong warrior, only to find myself drained with little victory to show for it. "Sit still and watch," ENOUGH whispered to me. "But I'm uncomfortable," I'd respond. "I know," she said softly, "it's okay."

I noticed NOT ENOUGH outside my windows shouting, calling, and begging for my attention. He could be very persuasive in inviting me outside my energy lane, prodding me to make a choice that did not align with my inner GPS. Sometimes, I couldn't control myself. I'd spend money on something to try and look important for someone else's approval, or I'd spout unsolicited advice to a friend as if I knew what it was to live in her reality.

There were other moments, too. Sometimes I sat. I let the discomfort, or even deep pain, be there. Sometimes, it washed out with the tide; sometimes, it pushed water out of my tear ducts; sometimes, it racked my body with sobs. But I sat, nonetheless. And even though I didn't celebrate with a victory parade, I felt less drained. I felt like I had more energy staying with me. I could use that increased energy to create and express and be and do. I tried more new stuff. I made more mistakes. I explored limits, boundaries, and values. And gradually, more often than not, I resisted the call to arms. I still hear NOT ENOUGH sometimes throwing rocks at the windows, but I generally have my music on so loud I barely notice. And sometimes, I crank the music all the way up to eleven and let it carry me away.

Nothing is solved, but I am increasingly more peaceful, more rested, and more gentled. I really do feel like I am learning to just be myself after all (shit, damn!).

Tricky Triggers

"I am so pissed. He totally gaslit me. I had prepared the P&L and all the financials, and instead of asking me questions, he looked to my male counterpart! I need a strategy for him to take me seriously." My client couldn't stop talking about the blatant misogyny she had just experienced on the job. I totally got it. Unfortunately, as a consultant, trainer, and executive coach, I have a front-row seat to so much injustice still alive and well in our workplaces. It happened. She saw it. She felt it. She got triggered.

The problem? She could labor for decades and still never get him to take her seriously. His bad behavior lived in his energy lane. As soon as she started stepping into his energy lane to fix him, she stepped out of her own. Even worse, the kind of human who gaslights another human is practically begging for you to join him in his energy lane; the gaslighter is selling you a product when you didn't even know you were shopping. Unconsciously, that was his agenda all along. He could get a hit of his own pseudo-power by dragging you from your lane into theirs.

My initial coaching and guidance fell on deaf ears. But after a few more instances, something clicked for her, and she readied herself for a new response. "Okay, I get it," she shared. "I'm wasting a lot of energy having fights with him in my head, and I'm drained and exhausted. How do I handle what happened and stay in my energy lane?"

I shared with her how to keep her power (okay, to fess up, ENOUGH used my voice to speak through me but no way would I explain that to my client). We set a strategy where she could notice the bad behavior and reflect on it without ever leaving her lane. Instead of revving up, she could get laser calm and simply observe the bad behavior with fierce self-care. Her response when it happened again was, "Hey (boss name hidden here), I noticed you were looking to Mark for the answer on that one. I think we may have some confusion as he didn't work with me on these financials. Is there something I can answer for you?" Bam! She shot her laser, and he stumbled. ENOUGH rode in her blazer pocket for the meeting, and with a little gentle encouragement, she had called out the toxic process without ever stepping outside her energy lane. She didn't deny her experience. In fact, she amplified it. But she disconnected the vacuum that had consistently pulled her out of her own lane and into his. She exhibited bullet-proof grace, a concept I love to teach to all my clients who tend to get overly stuck in others' drama.

These energy lane leaps occur just as often in personal relationships. NOT ENOUGH looooves to convince humans that if they only just do a little more and push a little harder, then the other person will be different. NOT ENOUGH sneaks into the earbuds with echoes of *maybe if you just do . . .* or *have you tried . . .* or *how about . . .* followed by loads of ideas that illustrate ways you can overgive, overserve, and do other people's jobs.

Their job? Be themselves. Your job? Stay out of their lane and do your own thing. But when NOT ENOUGH convinces you that you can be a hero, save the day, turn the company around, turn the leader around, fix the addiction, or any other of a thousand choices, you lose. Rather than enjoying your exploratory life path with ENOUGH, you lose sight of the possibilities. You hike along a path in the woods that keeps looping around to the trailhead. You feel like you are exploring, but you are simply revisiting the same territory, a foot over on the exact same hiking path. Sure, you might see some new wildlife with each pass, but the view never really changes. But when you stay in your energy lane, you discover mountains and rivers and vistas and countries and continents you may never have seen. You conserve your energy for your own hike rather than carrying someone else's gear on your back. You refuel with your own trail mix while allowing others to bring along their own rations.

But to be successful, we need to realize that we exited our energy lane in the first place. So how do you know? You feel like your guts are twisted into a rubber band wound up for a launch. You notice that although the players have changed, the situation seems very similar. You notice that you feel drained after certain interactions. You trip over your own superhero cape and stop listening to people who tell you that you can't change things. You get defensive in puffing yourself up to shut these people up. You feel a simmering but persistent rage. By the way, I am not saying you shouldn't make a stand, speak up, and incite change. Quite the opposite. If you let ENOUGH lead the way, while you stay in your energy lane, she'll show you countless ways to create an insurrection. And sometimes, the insurrection comes by quitting the game.

Saving vs. Serving

One of my favorite drugs of choice is rescuing (and NOT ENOUGH is the dealer). This drug comes in many flavors including saving, fixing, or even helping someone. I believe I have earned a gold medal in this category, both personally and professionally. I didn't understand until recently that saving, rescuing, and superheroing, in any way, creates a downhill runway out of my energy lane and into someone else's. I had crafted an identity of self-importance by helping other people. To be clear, I hope that the end of my days comes with an expansive sense of satisfaction in serving others. But it is a slippery slope between serving and saving. Service sometimes means drawing a strong boundary and saying, "I would love to help you, but that's really yours to do." Maybe you want to save your friend from a bad relationship, or your company from being unethical, or a child from making the mistakes you made. Whatever the reason, saving does not share space with ENOUGH.

ENOUGH reminds us that we have a role to play on the planet, and so does every being we meet. Our job is not to save them from themselves any more than it is their job to do that for us.

The early decades of my life were spent layering on personas of someone who could save the day—from fixing a printer to covering someone's bad behavior. But with a drug of choice, once I started, I couldn't stop. The first one's free, of course. But the second, third, fourth, and fiftieth came with a huge price tag. Over time, I became someone I had not intended. I lived in others' dramas with no time for my own story to unfold. Serving means setting someone up with the tools to succeed. Saving means using the tools for them. NOT ENOUGH always asks me to save the day. ENOUGH reminds me to save my energy for what most matters to me.

Playing My Own Game

If I spend my life confusing serving vs. saving I often land in a life I don't intentionally craft or create. My life becomes the default mode of my unconscious drive to matter. The more I learned to set boundaries and stay in my energy lane, ENOUGH kept inviting me on new paths. She refused to tell me which ones were the right ones or the wrong ones (which did piss me off for a while). Instead, she showed me landscapes in space, vast black voids, empty spaces of elegant nothingness that beckoned to me. At first, I was afraid. I had raised myself to believe in the terror of the black emptiness. I shied away from things I could not control or unpredictable endings. I completely missed the beauty of the dark, the mystery, the unknown—the blank canvases of creation. I spent a life pursuing the sunshine of the yang while missing the mystery of the yin. I didn't understand that creation takes place in the dark—sometimes the dark we experience in a still, quiet forest, and sometimes the dark, loud, noisy, cramped space of a womb birthing humans and possibilities. Either way, I continue to discover that innovation rarely somersaults off my clean, bright spreadsheets.

ENOUGH invited me to play my own game. When you play your own game, you trade in your pre-marked trails, the habits of stepping out of your energy lane, for the unexplored adventures of what could be.

———————

remember:

Stay in your energy lane.

CHAPTER 8

PROVING YOURSELF: NOT ENOUGH

WHO WILL BE AT THE EVENT? I BETTER MAKE SURE THEY KNOW HOW SUCCESSFUL I HAVE BEEN. DID SHE JUST MENTION MY AREA OF EXPERTISE? I BETTER MAKE SURE SHE UNDERSTANDS I HAVE DECADES OF EXPERIENCE IN THAT. THEY JUST TOOK MY IDEA, EXPANDED IT, AND POSTED IT ON THEIR WEBSITE. I BETTER MAKE SURE THEY REMEMBER I DID THAT FIRST.

"How is the business?" (them) "Great! I love working with executives. I have had the chance to coach a CEO of (namedrop company). I also work with C-level people who work in (namedrop industries) . . . I've been super busy, so it's kind of challenging right now (reverse brag by me)."

I'm staring at an empty mug of tea. My catching-up-with-a-friend-networking meeting wound itself down a few minutes ago, and only now, only in the aftermath of what appeared to be an outwardly normal conversation, could I feel his presence. NOT ENOUGH sneaked by the doorman when I wasn't looking.

One, two, three, cha, cha. Slow, slow, slow, quick, quick. Tap, tap, sway. *Pirouette*, back bend, step ball change, *pas de bourrée*, and shuffle off to Buffalo.

NOT ENOUGH loves to keep me dancing; the proving-myself polka tends to be his favorite.

The Sneak Attack

How had NOT ENOUGH snuck past? I am so glad you asked. A client I was working with had chosen not to do part two of a two-part engagement with me. He loved my work, but the required fee was not sustainable for their organization since they experienced a recent downturn in business. "I totally get it," I had commented to him on the phone.

My inner community should have been holding a ticker-tape parade in celebration. In the old days, if someone made a statement like this, I would have been slashing my prices like Walmart on Black Friday. If someone had mentioned a budget constraint, I would have immediately thrown on my super cape of unworthiness and said, "I'll help you out. Why don't I discount my services 75%?!!!" This time, I just held my space and acknowledged their situation by saying, "I totally get it." I should have been screaming from the rafters, "Way to go! You don't have to take every gig. You don't have to discount yourself. You don't have to over-give or over-deliver. You can walk away if something doesn't feel fun!"

And yet . . . And yet . . . And yet . . . I could still hear NOT ENOUGH yelling from his containment space, "See? I told you! You are not valuable. Who did you think you were, anyway, asking for that fee? You have gotten too big for your britches. You should be ashamed!" I could feel the shame lining the walls of NOT ENOUGH's cell in the small compartment in my belly.

All of this had occurred just before my networking coffee catch-up. To my chagrin, I turned that self-doubt into an Olympic sport of over-proving in what should have been relaxing chitchat.

This whole experience dragged me kicking and screaming into a deeper inquiry: who is the me who is working so hard to prove myself, and to whom?

ENOUGH never asks me to prove myself to her. In fact, she doesn't even understand the concept. When ENOUGH fills my space, I am struck by how precious I am, how special this little incarnation is, and how my very existence matters. I never feel the tug toward impressing when she's around. In fact, I usually spend the majority of my time telling others how much they matter, even when they think they are only a tiny speck on a big spinning orb.

As I began to survey the landscape of proving myself, I realized I play it out in many ways. Shall I underline how busy I am to prove how important I am? Yes! Shall I throw in some jargon while I'm at it? You bet! Shall I contort my brain to demonstrate a deeper or sharper insight than others in whatever career, industry, or topic we were discussing? Absolutely! I felt addicted to this behavior, often couched in normal expression with friends and acquaintances.

The insight had taken hold and wouldn't let go. I am an addict, I thought reflexively. I am addicted to proving my worth to others. Sometimes, I am overt. Sometimes, I am covert, but I live a carefully calculated existence of conversations and behaviors to tell you I am not only okay but that I am good, greater, or even better than you.

And yet, my addiction kept getting in the way of my joy. ENOUGH accepts every aspect of me as I am, with no changes. She demands nothing and gives everything. I slowly began to realize that the more time I spent working for others' endorsement, the more I stepped outside of my energy lane and lost my momentum to joy.

Throwing Egg on My Own Face

Arrrgh! My face smoked red hot with shame. We sat in our neighbor's backyard at a summer cookout at the end of the night. We had pulled our bag chairs up to the fire circle for the grown-ups-only chitchat while the kids filled up on cookies and sweets in the absence of any real parental oversight. I had just done that thing, that proving, that launching onto the runway of NOT ENOUGH to prove I mattered in some fashion, and as I juggled all of the eggs of self-importance very high in the air, one came crashing right back down on my face, a slimy mess that no one could miss.

I didn't know most of the people around the fire, and in an attempt to prove my value and importance, I had just shared a story. I had enjoyed the rare privilege of supporting a possible pilot TV episode that was being filmed (never did turn into anything). The gig was short-staffed, and I got to temporarily operate a camera with instructions from the seasoned professionals nearby. Rather than simply share how much fun I had because they let me dabble in their craft, I turned the story into a tale of superiority on how easy that job was.

I had all but finished when I quickly discovered that two of the people sitting around that fire were in the profession: a professional cameraman and a Director of Photography for film. Their credentials were long, and I had just made an ass of myself in an attempt to sound important. I had spoken about something I knew nothing about. I wanted to crawl out of my skin.

NOT ENOUGH loved to work through me by encouraging me to prove myself, to puff up my ego like a bag of chips readying for shipment. As usual, when NOT

ENOUGH operated in my life, it always ended badly. I had nowhere to run. I sat there and sucked up my stupidity and shame. These two humans were amazing, delightful, warm, authentic, and humble. I had immediately ruined any chance of two new friendships by my push to prove myself. I look back on what a wasted opportunity that was. Had I actually gotten to know them, I could have learned so much. Instead, I slung insults birthed of inferiority.

And yet, I'm still here. Nobody died. (I wish my ego would have!) I passed through the shame and came out on the other side a little wiser. I wish I could tell you that moment represented a turning point in my life where I stopped the scramble. Far from it. I continue to fall for the temptation more than I care to say. But then there is grace.

The more ENOUGH teaches me, the more I realize the level of grace she holds. She bears witness without judgment. She consoles and comforts in the worst of circumstances. And although shame often obscures my best thinking, I eventually take a breath and remember I have nothing to prove and notice that ENOUGH (and her grace) is always there.

––––––––

remember:

You have nothing to prove.

CHAPTER 9

EVEN WHEN YOU'RE NOT FEELING IT: ENOUGH

I AM NOT DOING WELL AT BEING A WIFE, A MOM, A FRIEND. IN FACT, I SUCK. I KNOW THE SUN IS BEHIND THE CLOUDS, BUT I FEEL THE HEAVINESS OF THOSE DAMN CLOUDS. WHAT IF EVERY ONE OF THOSE ENOUGH MOMENTS WAS A FLUKE? AN EXCEPTION? A FLEETING MOMENT? A LIE?

The best thing I can offer myself right now? A moment. A crack. A pause. An encouragement that hopefully, like the weather, this too shall pass.

These thoughts represented the best I could conjure up from within the haze of doubt. The thumbs beneath my suspenders often prop up a seeming space of wellness while I'm standing on a dung heap of my own thoughts.

Let's face it. Sometimes we don't have it. Maybe it was the hormones. Maybe the many small ouches of the week. Maybe the blood pressure or blood sugar reading that took me by surprise. Maybe the absorption of one more implied "I hate my mother" response from my child. I don't know, but sometimes I lose it. Actually, I don't just lose it; I lose any remnants of the scent on the trail.

ENOUGH does not fail me even then. No, she doesn't lift me up on angels' wings to soar across the expansive vista (although I am so down for that!) Instead, she sidles over and sits down next to me, our shoulders touching. She tells me that sometimes the best I can do is to choose a modicum of peace on the inside. Instead of dancing through life, I'm getting by with some pretty embarrassing moves. I may judge, but she doesn't judge. She tells me that even though I may be making all the wrong choices and even though NOT ENOUGH is hovering over me, ready to pounce and whip me into shape, she's quiet. She's calm. She's present. She reminds me that I'm simply living through another storm that eventually passes. And she graciously raises the limbo pole so I can slip underneath with the most minimal of efforts. She says, "Right now, let's just be a mess."

Outcast to Intimacy

Shit! Elbow to elbow, I sat sidled up to these powerhouse women. Business moguls, visionaries, forty under forties, the "connected," philanthropists, second home people. Women visioning a better world. Not perfect, but powerful.

ENOUGH invited me on this journey. She even warned me in advance, sat me down, and gave me a real talking-to. This time she took the form of a southern grandma I never had: "Honey," she said in a taffy-pulling voice that lulls you into a false sense of safety only to slap you upside the head, "you won't feel like you belong. You won't be comfortable. You may not have any value to add. You may not like it. But you're going!" I accepted the invitation to the conference. I engaged. I participated. I played. But I sat there at the end of the evening feeling less than worthy. A cold, dark night outside where NOT ENOUGH kept peeking in the windows of our casual gathering space. A stunning, stately woman and freshly published author who had just launched a second book sidled over and sat on the coffee table between me and a philanthropist. She commented on the missing glass of wine in my hand, another symbol of belonging I couldn't wear. I was nursing a small plastic bottle of conference-provided water while others were toasting the evening with more exciting libations.

Over the years, ENOUGH taught me that I didn't need to overshare. Sharing about my lifestyle choices did not represent openness but instead allowed NOT ENOUGH to get me chattering away to justify my values or even my existence. But tonight was different. ENOUGH, still sporting her southern grandma sass, blurted a reply to the woman's question about why I was holding the water . . . *recovering alcoholic* (me, that is). I paused and said nothing, feeling both satisfied and wondering if I had just thrown up on myself. Before I had a chance to overthink, the stately model burst into tears. She was supporting a cousin struggling with alcoholism. Tears sprung to my eyes. F*ck. Shit. Damn. ENOUGH. The philanthropist teared up, too, sharing that she'd been on a parallel journey with her son over the last handful of years.

The business chitchat quickly got to the real stuff among the three of us. The messiness, the struggles, the caring, the deep love, the beauty and the bullshit. I still don't know if that's the reason I was there or if there was more. But suddenly, none of it mattered. ENOUGH dropped her southern grandma persona and melted into me. Time slowed. Moments stretched. Others faded in the room. Here we were, the wise woman, the winner, and me . . . all opening our hearts to each other to be held in a precious pause. As we winded down our evening and talked about booze and sobriety and all the things that come with those ideas, we let our masks fall to the floor. We cried and talked for over an hour! I walked to my hotel room that night with an expanded heart, feeling bigger. What started out as a series of awkward meetings where I faked my way through all the social stuff, had turned into a treasure of a night. ENOUGH does that somehow. When she inhabits you, you expand. You are bigger than your body, larger than your life circumstances, and inspired to irrational levels.

So no, I don't always feel ENOUGH's presence, but she never leaves. Sometimes, I leave myself, but I have never fully lost her. She might be hiding in a stranger's coat or a cup of tea or in the voice of a friend, but she always comes back. She sits with me so that I know I am here, that I exist, that I matter, and that . . . in the end, even when I am not feeling it, all is well.

Handbag Hell

[Order now]. Click. Momentary delight hit my heart as I clicked submit to order a handbag I had looked at and researched, which was also an "it" bag of the year. I could argue that it fit my new mindset of only buying quality items that would last a long time—clothes and items that fit me now and fit me forever. My thinking that a few carefully selected very high-quality items, not a lot of them, just a few, would be my mainstay. I had discarded garbage bags of items to get simple and small. I could justify my handbag purchase with that in mind, but that wouldn't be honest. I had looked at this bag. I liked it. But I walked away because it was more than I felt like spending, and I liked it but didn't love it.

On that early morning, when I woke up and was unable to go back to sleep, a tagalong ad for the bag followed me, and I looked at it again. It was out of stock everywhere. The previous walk away had turned into a drive to find it somewhere, anywhere, which I eventually did. One site had it in stock in the color I wanted for a reasonable price. I clicked submit. But I hadn't really made the purchase for me. I made it on the ladder of comparison. I thought about how impressed people "who knew" would be if they saw my bag. The purchase would solidify my place on that rung or maybe the rung above. Sure, I knew that, at the top of the ladder, the bag had no value. Those humans could buy dozens, but at my rung, it was impressive. The bag wasn't for me. I ordered the bag in a misguided attempt to hold a spot on the ladder or climb further up, but I had tried that in the past. It never worked. I'd step up a rung only to find out that my choice no longer mattered at the new rung.

Worse still, I felt deep shame by my choice. How could I have made that purchase even though I knew better? ENOUGH had me writing this book. I knew I wasn't orienting to my values. NOT ENOUGH was racing through my veins like a drug—fast, reckless, short-lived, and inviting a bigger crash. I felt very down. But luckily, ENOUGH had done more than a drive-by in my life. She had begun visiting pretty regularly. Like a friend who comes over and listens to you unburden your heart when you make a mistake, she wrapped her arm around me and sent me here to share with you. Even though I wasn't "feeling it," was not orienting to my internal GPS, was having difficulty feeling ENOUGH's presence, and was leaping onto the ladder of comparison, she did not join my shame party.

In living with ENOUGH I imagined a new world, a solid state, a space where I wouldn't be slipping back into my former ways of being. But with her hand on my back, ENOUGH reminded me that her way does not mean perfection. In fact, she runs from perfection. Living with ENOUGH means being real, being authentic, telling it like it is, sharing when you're an asshole. Living with ENOUGH means not defending stupid moves. Living with ENOUGH means saying, "Damn, I regret that. I screwed up. I made a mistake. I'm sorry."

Living with ENOUGH means stepping into the great chasm, the one that invites us to imagine the possibility that we might be unconditionally loved by someone, somewhere, somehow. Living with ENOUGH does not mean believing I am precious all of the time; it means shopping the concept.

I don't know what divine love, G-d, or any of those things really are. I only know that the little desperate girl who inhabits the core of my being hopes beyond hope that a force truly exists that loves us unconditionally. My eyes are wet with the simple idea of it, the idea that right now, right here in this very moment, with all of my desires, shortcomings, and imperfections, there might be no problem at all, nothing to fix, nothing to do. It is possible that I am not only loved, but I *am* love, that I chose to play in this living-on-the-earth experience to simply feel things, to experience, to choose to be human.

Ironically, the company canceled the handbag order. "Out of Stock!" the email notice told me. Maybe I'm naive, but I think ENOUGH made some magic on my behalf. (I told you she was getting sassier.)

When Your Best is Where You Are Right Now

"I feel like I just want to be more connected. I know intellectually we have a limited amount of time. I have always known that to some degree. I'm sixty. I'm thinking I'll live to a maximum of 90 or 85 or 70. Maybe I have until the end of the year, I don't know. The point is I want to just be more relaxed, be more okay. It is this scrambling. It is the scrambling all the time externally as if I'm not enough, as if I were only a better person, then I'd be ten pounds lighter, and I'd always brush the damn dogs' teeth every night, and my money would always be in great shape, and I'd always be on top of everything, on top of my kids' needs and my job's requests even though it would be impossible because you always get more than you could do. My sleep would be impeccable. My wardrobe would be . . . I don't know. And you know it's like, damn it! There is all that stuff to manage, but it is also my

*internal state. I am really trying to claim that I am okay and that I'm enough. Even now, as I say that, I can feel myself slowing down. There is no perfect way to do it. This is my best today, and I don't feel super focused, and I don't know why. I kind of wish this Monday were another Sunday. I would like to cook or read or just sit. But I have done the things I really needed to do, so I am going to let it go and find my mojo and go at it the next day. I'm not there yet mentally, but I just want to be working on this. I have to wonder. When I'm dead, will it matter that I did every day f*cking perfectly? No! So, why? Why am I putting all this pressure on myself?."*

This beautiful, wonderful rant wiggled its way into my voicemail from a dear friend. ENOUGH had gotten quite entitled over time, and she'd stopped with the subtleties. She not only talked to me through my thoughts but through others' words. I listened to this voicemail and wanted to cry as it might as well have been me expressing myself (minus the dogs—I don't have any).

I let myself tear up while I walked and listened to the voicemail. I let myself be embraced by her transformation with ENOUGH's influence in under two minutes during a voicemail message. Nothing changed in her outside circumstances. NOT ENOUGH still masqueraded through the silent screaming needs of the dog, the spouse, the job, and the kids, but my friend didn't take the bait. She noticed the pull. She noticed herself tap dancing on his game board, and then she leaped off, right into the arms of ENOUGH.

ENOUGH did not solve anything. She didn't fix anything. She simply allowed my friend to slow down for a short pause, to ask the small but potent questions that allowed her heartbeat to rest, to introduce a glitch in NOT ENOUGH's Las Vegas neon light distraction reality. My friend turns her eyes to the forest. A small pause for her, a big win for her soul.

Not a Pollyanna or a Pushover

"This sucks!" I looked squarely into the eyes of my friend, who was dying of breast cancer. Usually, this friend tends to be a bit prim and proper, but she leaned in, grabbed my hand, and angrily blurted the echo, "This sucks!" I suppose I could have offered another sweeter or more comforting response, but it would have been complete and utter BS.

Through this whole exchange, ENOUGH held my waist. She held me from the moment my eyes brimmed with tears to the point that those tears dragged my mascara down my face leaving deep tracks. In all my times with ENOUGH, she never asked me to feel any particular way. ENOUGH never tells me to *just cheer up* or *look on the bright side!* I don't know if she supports everyone this way or knows I would punch her if she threw these trite phrases my way, but I don't think her approach is special to me. ENOUGH has held my hand through righteous outrage, deep sadness, and complete elation. Unlike me, she doesn't seem to ride the coaster up or down with any of these states. She sits in the stillness, bearing witness. ENOUGH is neither a Pollyanna nor a pushover. She probably witnesses the horror as well as the bliss. She sometimes holds my hand or my heart, and sometimes I have a really difficult time knowing she exists at all. But she never tells me to feel anything other than what I feel. She never tells me to be anyone other than who I am. She never tells me to do anything other than what I am doing. She simply is.

Despite the catastrophic situation, despite not having an easy onramp, I was increasingly learning to *be*, even in the tough times. "I am just depressed," another friend had claimed over coffee that same week. "I hear you. I am so sorry," I replied. I'd love to claim credit for this simple, honest response, but it was really ENOUGH's influence that led me to abandon any advice, insights, or strategies. I had been there myself. I still go there sometimes. ENOUGH gave me permission to be depressed, and the least I could do was offer that same favor to others.

———

remember:

You won't always be able to feel or hear ENOUGH. That is just fine.

CHAPTER 10

DENY, DISMISS, AND DIMINISH: NOT ENOUGH

DON'T YOU THINK YOU ARE OVERREACTING? ARE YOU SURE YOU ARE NOT BEING OVERLY SENSITIVE? THAT'S NOT THE WAY I SAW IT. WELL, THERE ARE TWO SIDES TO EVERY STORY, AREN'T THERE?

"He told me I'm no longer a candidate because I lack ambition. They are now looking for external candidates." This woman executive shared the results of her evaluation to be the next CEO of her company. She was the only internal candidate for the role. "He also said I need to work on not being so overpowering." As an executive coach, my job is to be impartial, to listen, to hear, to feel, to travel with, and to always look at what skills the executive needs for the next phase of their leadership. But sometimes, I completely lose my shit. I lost my shit.

My client had worked for the company for over fifteen years, and her skills in doing whatever it took to drive results, while also developing people and teams, were fairly unprecedented in her space. Usually, executives were good at one or the other and had to fill in their team with the skills they did not possess. She was highly gifted in polar opposite areas: strong IQ and EQ. Her entire career reflected ambition. She had overcome significant obstacles, completed turnarounds, and delivered results. Her people loved her. I had just completed her 360 feedback interviews, and one employee said, "I'd follow her anywhere." That quote summarized her entire team's view of her leadership.

Yet here we were, conversing about a fabricated reality of complete nonsense. The current CEO and stakeholders could not picture a woman leading the company who was both direct and caring, strong and soft. They felt threatened about what her leadership might mean to them and their future board positions. Fortunately, they didn't have to reflect very long. NOT ENOUGH had been joining their golf outings and happy hours and had laid out a complete strategy, a plan that allowed them to avoid their fears and discomfort. Why not bring in an outside consultant to evaluate? Let's give her a battery of assessments we have never had to take ourselves so we can gather loads of data to create a narrative where Deny, Dismiss, and Diminish can have a field day with her.

The Emperor Has No Clothes

NOT ENOUGH can't stand alone. He has no actual feet, so others need to prop him up. NOT ENOUGH's good buddies often take on this role. The Deny, Dismiss, and Diminish triplets often travel together, hang in the same circles, and try (unsuccessfully) to drive out ENOUGH.

In this case, NOT ENOUGH had sent out his henchmen, and my client joined our coaching session in a tailspin: *"Am I crazy?"* she lamented. *"Didn't I consistently exceed the numbers and goals quarter by quarter, year by year? Maybe my employees don't think I'm that great. Do I need to be more ambitious?"*

I felt ENOUGH rise up to speak through me. The client and I painstakingly walked back through her history, her 360 results, and the company's metrics. Eventually, through the lens of our online meeting, I saw ENOUGH settle into my client's lap. Her breathing moved from fast and ragged to calm and regulated. She remembered who she was. She would go on to be a great CEO, just not at this company.

I want to say I was happy at her realization, but I was mostly relieved. Deny, Dismiss, and Diminish had gone in for a bloodbath but had walked away hungry. I completely saw myself in my client that day.

What's Your Problem?

"I don't think it was that bad," she said. My facade was a serene mask, but beneath it, a storm raged. Like an animal baring its teeth, I flashed what appeared to be a tight smile, but it was simply me opening my jaw to release a breath. The tension in my posture spoke volumes, but she didn't notice. I was a predator ready to pounce. A group of friends and I had experienced a trauma, and I was sharing my feelings with one of the friends who wasn't directly involved but had stood nearby. "I don't think it was that bad," was her response to my outrage at what happened to us. Clearly, the DDD triplets showed up to the conversation.

I understood what was going on. She needed to deny, dismiss, and diminish my experience. If she had acknowledged the truth, she would have had to sort out and come to terms with her own experience, her choice not to act and not to digest what had happened. She was not ready to do that. She might never be.

I experienced our conversation both as a participant and observer. I heard the score of the music before it came out of her mouth, but I had a hard time escaping my rage. Too often in my life, I would have avoided difficulties, but ENOUGH had moved into serious training mode. I learned that the more I felt her inside me, the more outrageous I could be, and the more I could upset the apple cart to be on my own side. I was proud of the choices I had made to tell the truth about my experience from my own perspective without apology.

Dance Party or Dance-Off

I am not sure about this as a universal truth, but my most expansive experiences are often followed by some of the deepest doubts or despairs. I quickly learned that the more I befriended ENOUGH, the more NOT ENOUGH freaked out, flailing on the floor like a two-year-old in a tantrum. At these times, NOT ENOUGH resorted to these extreme measures, like bringing along the posse of Deny, Dismiss, and Diminish.

Sometimes, I make a big move—a move backed by ENOUGH's quiet boldness—and I expect, in that space of joy, others to surround me and celebrate me because of my courage. I expect a chorus of hallelujahs to ring out and celebrate my new liberation and sense of worthiness. And yes, I sometimes have that experience when my headphones are on, and I am listening to my music without the interference of anyone else's opinions. With my headphones on, I can't deny the beat. *Truth, express. Truth, express. Truth, express.* My legs come alive to this fabulous rhythm, and I eagerly layer on some improv. What I think and feel inside finally reflects what I say and do outside. Oh, joy! Oh, glory! I get a sense of my limbs and inhabit my skin.

I enjoy these big expansions when they come. ENOUGH may beam out from my inner core, demonstrating the possibilities for others as they watch me dance to my rhythm. I may even notice a few individuals tentatively place a toe on the same proverbial dance floor. I may eagerly look forward to them joining me in our big group number that's sure to come. In my vision, they join me in the rule-breaking, gift-sharing, truth-telling, stand-making, wild freedom of being authentic.

But that doesn't always happen. Sometimes I am taken by surprise as I watch others watching me. NOT ENOUGH stands in front of these individuals, arms crossed, blocking their path to the dance floor. I can almost see their insides moving to their unique beat, but their outsides keep tap dancing. Their insides beat *truth, express. Share, contribute.* But their outsides flail wildly. Deny, Dismiss, Diminish. Deny, Dismiss Diminish.

I can easily get confused by their rhythm. I may keep trying to teach them the beat. "Hey," I exclaim, "don't worry. The dance of being yourself is actually way easier than I thought. Two easy steps in this part! Truth. Express."

But they keep moving erratically . . . on the dance floor, off the dance floor, on the dance floor, off the dance floor. Clap. Clap. Clap. Deny, Dismiss, Diminish. *Truth? Express?* Clap. Clap. Clap. Deny, Dismiss, Diminish.

My dance can falter as I look for them to join me. After all, this was shaping up to be a flash mob, wasn't it? I hadn't planned on a solo after all. But the more I stand near them, the more I lose my beat. I talk about vision, but there they are, repeating the chants of Deny, Dismiss, and Diminish. I argue even more strongly, and the louder I get, the louder their chants echo back.

I may begin to doubt my own experience. I have now formally invited Doubt as a fourth D to this party of insanity. I wonder, did that really happen? Maybe I was wrong. Maybe I made up that beat. Did I misunderstand? Is there a master soundtrack that everyone is tuned to but I can't hear? And with every self-doubt, my feet get tangled. I stumble on the dance floor. I wonder if I should grab a seat.

Deny, Dismiss, and Diminish come out in full force to party with their friend, NOT ENOUGH, who has made his grand entrance.

The more ENOUGH put me through her training, the more I noticed the options in these situations. I often expected, hoped, and inappropriately wished for others to join me, but that wasn't their choice and it wasn't my journey. The possibilities fanned out before me.

I could take a seat. I see a chair in the corner, off the stage. I could watch from that position and not make an ass of myself. I could journal about the rhythm I momentarily felt. I could make a vision board about it. That feels safer. But the more I entertain these new thoughts, and the more the triplets push me off the dance floor, the angrier I sometimes get. I like my rhythm, I think. I hear those beats. I did NOT make that up. I like dancing. I will not be shoved off the floor. Then it hits me.

Yes, I had been dancing to my rhythm of Truth, Express, and Dare, but I hadn't noticed all the strings I had attached.

I had chosen to enjoy the company of ENOUGH, but only if . . .

No one doubted me.

No one challenged me.

I never encountered Deny, Dismiss, and Diminish.

That insight forced my hand on my journey. I leaped from my imaginary chair in the corner and stepped onto my stage, the one without the audience and the clapping admirers. I struck a pose in the spotlight of my own making, found my internal rhythm, and danced like no one was watching.

ENOUGH thrives without her strings. ENOUGH sings Kenny Rogers as I sit in the coffee shop reminding me, "You've got to know when to hold 'em. Know when to fold 'em. Know when to walk away. Know when to run."

In the movement of my own dance, I run from NOT ENOUGH and fall into the arms of ENOUGH. Suck on that . . . triple Ds.

———————

remember:

Deny, Dismiss, and Diminish show up because you are doing so well. Pay them no mind.

CHAPTER 11

SLOWING DOWN TO THE SPEED OF LIFE: ENOUGH

The more ENOUGH became a part of my life, the more I slowed down to experience the many joys I had been missing. I was almost overwhelmed by the many meaningful moments that began to pile up in a short timeframe of being, existing, living, and experiencing.

Unlikely Airline Experiences

Stuck on the runway at the Charlotte airport in a full shutdown after the two-hour delay in Asheville, with a flashing red light signaling full airport closure and darkened planes with passengers littering the taxiways, lightning taunted us from all around our 360 views to let us know the end of our adventure would not be arriving anytime soon. In fact, we would be held in limbo for quite a while to come. I typed this entry in my online journal:

Maybe I should be cranky, but I don't care!!! Angels guard my every step, and I am completely tended to. I think new adventures are unfolding, and I don't know how or when they'll work, but I'm delighted that they are exceeding my expectations. Who would have thought this was what I needed?

How did I land in this zen space amid hundreds of cranky passengers, road-weary flight attendants, and crying babies? Sitting in a cubicle in the corner of the airport working on my laptop, I keep checking my airline app because my seat on the first leg of the flight kept changing: back one row, then back a few more rows, then moved from an aisle to a window. I scarcely hear my name being called over a gargled intercom urgently commanding me to report to the gate.

I make a quick last-minute prayer as I shove the cords and electronics in my leather backpack and pick my way through a mass of sprawled travelers, dodging bags and outstretched legs, avoiding accusing looks on weary faces.

At the desk, they let me know that the airline had pushed our original flight back *so late* that they decided to move everyone to an earlier flight so we could make our connections in Charlotte. I grab my freshly printed boarding pass, and sure enough, my seat is now even further back and not on the aisle. The paper ticket shows the flight boarding in a few minutes, so I hang out near the desk, queuing up for boarding group six on a very tiny plane.

Strangely, almost no one stands up as they call groups one, two, three, four, or five, so I am still early in the boarding crowd. Just as the gate attendant is about to scan my pass, she pulls it away from me and says, "I'm so sorry, these seats keep shifting; you have a new pass." I barely glance at the ticket, assuming I am now in a non-reclining seat in the very last row of the plane next to the cupboard bathroom. But to my surprise and shock, the new pass shows me in the third row of first class! Without saying a word (out of fear that the entire transaction would quickly be discovered for the massive error it was), I make my way down the ramp, boarded, and settled in—window seat, row three!

As other passengers board, I spend way too much time thinking, trying to reason out the logic. How did I manage to get bumped up? I had a less-than-zero status on the airline. Did I accidentally press a button to pay for an upgrade on my app without realizing it? I double-check it, but I have not. The airline combined two flights, which usually means more passengers with priority status fighting over who is more important for the few available seats. My thoughts are interrupted as another woman, who has also been upgraded, takes the seat next to me. Unlike me, she seems a bit cranky and . . . sad? I notice her talking to another passenger and making her way down the aisle, and it dawns on me that she is separated from her friend or sister or family member.

An outrageous urge bubbles up in my heart-gut, and before I think too much about it, I blurt out, "Do you want to have your friend take my seat?" My head brain registers its displeasure immediately in the angry chorus of my thoughts. *Are you nuts? You were pushed to the back, and now you have this great seat, and there have been huge delays. Are you giving up the third-row first class?!!!*

My seatmate, slightly surprised by my comment but also looking down at me like I might be a little stupid, shoots back, "My friend is in 13C . . . *not* first class." Ironically, row 13 was my original row before all of the seat shuffling. "I know," I reply, working hard to ignore the clawing of my mind trying to get my attention over my heart-gut. She grabs her mobile to call her friend and ask, but her friend isn't picking up. They are loading passengers quickly to try and take off before an airport shutdown.

"Why don't you go and ask her?" I say. She gets up and starts pushing down the aisle to find her friend. When she finally comes back with a solid yes, I flag down the flight attendant to let her know I'm switching seats. She had just handed me a paper cup with some hot water for tea, and

I didn't want her to be thrown off when I disappeared. Befuddled, she looks at me and, just like my seatmate, tries to educate me firmly but quickly, "But that's not first class!!" "I know," I respond. By now, I'm having a ton of fun responding to people who are talking to me like I am a complete idiot who doesn't speak English.

It is too late for rationality. The excitement I feel shooting through my veins is now a drug I can't quite get enough of. After a little more confusion, she tells me to hang on. I'm waiting for her to return and scold me like my second-grade nun teacher, to belittle me for the choice I have made that inconveniences her. Instead, she returns, and still keeping what I perceive as a schoolmarm tone, she directs me to move to another seat now. I hop up and move to where she directs me, to the first row of first class!!!! No one is there in the entire row. I try to settle in but can't completely unwind because I'm still waiting for the other shoe to drop, for that special passenger to board, the one who should be in my seat.

Eventually, she rotates the airlock door and seals it with that final sigh, which means no one else is getting on even if they try. I am trying to sort out the body sensations I'm experiencing. The urge that started with a rush of adrenaline now settles itself in and spreads through my entire nervous system . . . a sensation of warmth and hugs from grandma and chocolate chip cookies and rainbow sparkles shooting from unicorn butts.

ENOUGH not only showed up. This time, she came wearing spandex and tiaras and waving her cape. ENOUGH had stepped right into that otherwise bad, cranky, inconvenient, over-crowded, flight-delayed day. She invited me to jump, and I said yes.

The rest of the flight continued to present apparent obstacles at every turn. Our flight stayed on that tarmac for several more hours before departing. The woman one row back on the opposite side desperately begged for just one more plastic cup of straight-up booze, and my heart broke at the familiar signs of the successful alcoholic executive who learned to cover their desperation in social settings. ENOUGH inside me kept expanding my empathy. I talked with one of the flight attendants about her grandchild. She sat down in the seat next to me for a long while in those couple hours, a much more comfortable spot than her awkward jump seat. I applauded the other attendant who had just come back from trying to comfort and entertain a cranky baby and mom in the back.

Eventually, we took off from Asheville and landed in Charlotte. They had already closed the doors for the Charlotte to Chicago flight, but miraculously, they did what they never do . . . reopened the doors for a group of us looking desperate to get home.

When they loaded us, I made my way to the back of this flight . . . a flight filled with people who had sat on their tarmac for hours and clearly had nothing left. But nothing could bring me down from my high. I enjoyed being smashed into this can of humanity. I loved watching the young girl next to me watching the same anime show on her iPad that my son watched. But then the real pain began.

In front of me, a young toddler would not stop screaming. I could hear the strain in the voice of the very tired, very young mom who was close to screaming at her son to tell him to shut up. I could tell she was not a violent mom. I would bank on the fact that, on most days, she probably acted super chill. But her son wouldn't stop, and many passengers kept giving her very dirty looks as if she were intentionally holding the magic rest potion from her son so that he would torture them. I have been in those shoes before, and it hurts.

I thought back to when my son, borderline colicky as a baby, would not stop scream-crying. I finally understood how mothers could accidentally shake their babies to death. (If you are a mom and can't relate, hop down off your high horse and be grateful you haven't had to live through the experience. A friend whose child did the same told me once, "I wanted to peel the wallpaper off the walls with my fingernails!")

I chose not to intervene on the flight. I could offer to hold her son, but even if that worked, which was unlikely, she'd just feel inadequate as a mom anyway. We finally took off, and she strained her way through the couple-hour flight back home. When we unloaded, and I was walking off the plane, I made my way to the side of the exit path in the terminal where she and Grandma were working to get the baby into the stroller. He had, by now, stopped crying. Walking down the ramp back into the terminal, I stopped to tell her that my son had sometimes had a hard time with not crying, and I reassured her that she was a really good mom. Grandma looked me straight in the eye and said, "She needs to hear that." I told her that I thought her son was expressing all of the crankiness for the whole plane, that as adults, we learn to bottle everything up inside, but as a baby, he doesn't have that filter. She thanked me, her eyes brimming with tears.

Sensing how important it was for her to hear this again, I turned back one more time to say, "You're a really good mom. You are doing great!" Now, you may hear this story and mistakenly think I did something good for her. You wouldn't be wrong, but you wouldn't be fully right. With ENOUGH as my fellow traveler that day, I was receiving way more than I was giving. The thought that struck me on this particular day was, *this is it. This is what I looove to do for a living.* I love to care, to connect, to understand, to feel with, and to help if I can. And I love to feel the warmth of mattering as it inevitably flows through my system. This day was before I had fully set up my company. I was dreaming and visioning but hadn't yet made so many dreams come true. That was still to come. But my relief in finding my new living, my new calling, was huge. I realized from then on that I would do all kinds of things for money. But I knew that every single one of those "jobs" was really just a vehicle for my real job. And my real job could be done in endless ways every day with ENOUGH by my side.

And this wasn't the "I'll give up everything I have so you can have whatever you need" kind of pseudo-altruistic BS. Quite the opposite. More like the "I am selfishly going to go for what delights me and brings me joy no matter what, and oh, by the way, when I do that, I get to experience the high that comes in giving out a sense of huge overflow, because I have taken up residence with ENOUGH and she is the best roommate I have ever had.

The Gift Lives with the Giver

Her gratitude significantly outweighed the gesture. I had just helped an older woman open a locked door to the church on the corner as I was walking home. I identify more as Hobbit than human, and she looked half my height as she shuffled her walker along the sidewalk, moving toward me. She used the walker to move, but its limbs also held various plastic bags filled with what I assume were necessities for the day. When she turned her walker in the direction of the church's side door, I reached to open the door but discovered it was locked. She had keys and enthusiastically welcomed my help turning the key while pulling the heavy door.

She poured her gratitude over me with an abundance that far outweighed the small act. She expressed the delight of a kid on Christmas morning. I lost count of how many times she thanked me. I felt slightly sad that the small act might have been an exception in her day.

The transaction lasted less than five minutes, yet her thankfulness bathed me the rest of the day. Her sunshine beams of gratitude warmed me to the core. I felt valuable, important, and needed. As I walked away, I realized how much she had given me. Before that, I was lost in a tangle of distracted thoughts, including whether or not I had added enough value during a client meeting. After meeting her, nothing in my brain tangle mattered at all.

I've heard it said that *it is better to give than to receive.* I always put a moral framework on that, an implied "should" to the giving. With this woman, it struck me hard. I benefit far more as the giver than the receiver. So, thank you to the woman whose name I don't know who gave me the priceless gift of profound mattering. I wish you back one thousandfold what you gave to me.

Life on the Asphalt

What is he doing? Is he okay? Four friends and I had been enjoying our time on a work/writing/relaxing trip in upstate New York. A day after we arrived at our cabin, they began resurfacing the asphalt on the road outside. The first construction crew we passed seemed pretty inept, and I was a little concerned we might be hit by an oncoming car, but we made it to the main road, where they were doing even more work.

After coming to a full stop to let the other lane pass, we were finally moving and approaching the man holding the slow/stop sign. But something wasn't right. He was flailing and gyrating all over the place. *Is he okay?* I wondered as we neared. Not really understanding what was going on until we got closer, I had thoughts running through my mind like . . . are his coworkers noticing this man is having a seizure? I was clearly seeing the world through some pretty warped glasses. This construction worker with bare arms and the dayglow vest was dancing his ass off! Talk about ENOUGH! The 90-degree heatwave clearly hadn't halted his choice to fully express himself in what others may have considered a boring, hot, difficult job.

ENOUGH leaped onto my lap even though I was driving. As we approached, I did my best to match his dance gyrations from the driver's seat of the car, and so did my co-pilot. The flagman nodded and saluted as we danced and drove on by. We passed him two more times during our trip, and both times, ENOUGH made sure I seat-danced our greeting, which brought a delightful response from him.

Thanks to ENOUGH's vitality for life, we could savor the heart delight that emerged from a dance with a stranger on the road. We were anonymous women driving by in a non-descript minivan. He was a random roadside worker doing the daily grind. Together, for three brief instants, we experienced each other more deeply.

Street Encounter: A Blessing in a Quarter of a Block

The hunched man with the cane caught my attention as I got out of my car to walk to the evening event. The neighborhood could be dicey, I thought, as he clearly made intentional eye contact with me. When no "spidey senses" tingled, I felt a subtle urge to make contact. His slow pace timed him perfectly to be right next to my car as I shut the door. I shut the door just as he struck up the conversation, "Do you know what's in that place?" He motioned toward one of the brownstone, two-flat buildings. It looked closed up but had an artistic creation hanging over the door, a sign often marking the beginnings of gentrification. "I don't," I replied. "A group of guys came over here the other day," he shared, "and they were tossing bags of trash up there. I tried to get them to stop. Instead, they went through all my pockets to take anything they could find. Now, if I see them, I just cross the street." This gentle soul, I learned as I took mini steps to keep pace with him and walk the quarter block to the event entrance, was on his way to the doctor. Shortly, he'd be catching the express bus. My heart ached imagining a group of guys roughing him up and going through his pockets. We exchanged a few words in what became a micro-moment of my lifetime.

I said goodbye to him when I reached the entrance to the event. He kept walking but not before shouting, "God bless you!" And I did allow myself to accept and receive the blessing from him. He had blessed me, and I think I had blessed him too. *"Fellow passengers to the grave,"* the quote from Dicken's *A Christmas Carol* struck me then. In a small, tiny breath of humanity, he saw me, I saw him, and we shared a meaningful exchange before we both went our separate ways. That's the treasure. That is the gold. No financial transaction. No ask of each other. Just a recognition, an honoring of what it is to choose to be a human, standing next to each other with the awareness of coexisting. ENOUGH. Without trappings or agendas, ENOUGH stood between us, joining our hands in what I can only describe as a simple but deeply moving exchange. I stood in my energy lane during that moment. Warmth washed over me. I was inspired, beautifully still in a wash of gratitude.

Worshipping False Gods

With ENOUGH, I was slowing down to the speed of life, not the speed of life's expectations or distractions or hustle.

Those were NOT ENOUGH's doing. I was learning that NOT ENOUGH's world was abundant with the worship of false gods. In another decade of my life, I may have avoided the man with the cane. I may have driven past the construction worker with an odd look on my face, wondering about his recreational drug use. I would have joined the mass of crankiness at the airports. Instead, I was slowing down to the speed of life's possibilities, of the joy available in the little moments. And to be clear, slowing down doesn't mean you need to physically slow down. For me, slowing down happens when I allow ENOUGH to take the wheel. She has an uncanny ability, with the turn of a dial, to slow down the progression of time so that the moment stretches to more than a moment. As time stretches, I am able to enjoy the kind of joy, delight, and meaning normally reserved for transcendent experiences or for close family and friends and their milestones. With ENOUGH, I can experience that delight with a random passenger on a plane or a dancer on the road.

———————

remember:

Give yourself permission to slow down to the speed of life.

CHAPTER 12

THE POSSIBILITIES

"GOOOOOOD MORNING!!!!!!" the spry woman in her seventies sped by me on her bike, shouting and waving her very boisterous and borderline aggressive greeting with the dynamite-packed enthusiasm only a high school cheerleader can muster.

That morning, I decided to go for a wander. The slow wander. A peaceful walk, the "feels good to get my steps in, but I'm not counting" kind of wander along the lake. On my way back, along the bike path, this white-haired dynamo had blurred past, assaulting me with her joy. She rocketed past me, excitedly greeting every single person along the path. I giggled as I passed the other recipients of her unsolicited love. Like me, they acted serious, but you couldn't miss the tell-tale upturned mouth corners fighting back grins.

I hadn't quite experienced ENOUGH unleashing this wildly, speeding by and launching joy bombs with the enthusiasm of a basketball mascot blasting their T-shirt cannonballs at halftime. Except in this case, each one of us caught the prize.

I kept watching my new elderly friend until I noticed her stop to talk to a park district worker driving a truck on the path. I shifted my course from the walking path to intentionally reroute and get on her bike path. I had missed the chance to get to know this wonderful human during her first drive-by, and I wanted a second chance.

As I approached the yellow municipal truck, I saw that the woman and the worker were deep in conversation. I clearly overhead enough conversation snippets that I knew they had made contact multiple times in the past. Not wanting to disturb their intimacy, I kept walking, secretly hoping that she'd pass me again so I could stop her. Five or ten minutes passed as I kept walking with no sign of her coming up from behind. I had just given up and was turning off the trail toward home when I saw her speeding toward me again. This time, I was prepared. I waved wildly and greedily at her to stop and talk to me.

As a side note, I would never, ever, ever have done such a thing before ENOUGH came into my life. I'd dismiss the experience or maybe share it as a funny anecdote with a friend later in the afternoon. But I truly hadn't met anyone since my journey had begun who bubbled over with so much ENOUGHness, and I absolutely had to know her.

Of course, she stopped. When you brim with ENOUGH, when you know her so intimately, you have time for any human who wants to share and make contact. I asked her point blank, "What is your story? I love your energy. How did this come to be?"

Meet Phyllis. Phyllis graciously shared her tale: how she had gotten a very severe ailment in her leg that, "at my age, should have killed me." Once she realized she'd make it through, she figured she had a purpose to be on the planet. She had decided to live every day in this joyous fashion. As we talked, others passed on the path and greeted her, and she greeted them back. Many of these early morning path people clearly knew her and felt warmly toward her. She attributed her healing to a miracle of G-d, and she couldn't wait to share herself with anyone who would have her. I was really struck by her. Her eyes twinkled. Her skin was radiant. Her body was youthful. Her energy was infectious.

I began to wonder about the ripple effect of her sharing. A good-sized crew filled those paths every morning. She had been doing the good morning ride for quite a while. I feebly attempted to do the multiplication of impact in my mind before surrendering.

And what did she have? A bike? A voice? A daring to look wonderfully ridiculous? My collision with her shifted my entire experience that day. When I finally made my way home, I internally blessed everyone I passed. (No—I haven't yet graduated from conformity in a way that I shout enthusiastically to strangers, but stay tuned; anything is possible). When I finally got home, I took a bath and savored my soak. Later, I fielded a call from a troubled friend, and she praised and thanked me for being so calm and clear. I went on to work that day doing consulting and networking, all with an enlivened heart. A small gift of her shared joyous humanity had, at a minimum, uplifted and inspired me for at least eighteen hours.

So, what's possible then? What if, rather than defending myself at a critique from my husband, I just let it be there? What if I released the people I judged and criticized and knew their choices weren't my job? What if we all did? What if that insecure executive I knew didn't try to manipulate because of their sense of inferiority? What if that young woman loved her body and took care of it vs. abusing it under the guise of an unreachable beauty standard? What if those two people with polar opposite views remembered they were both humans who cared?

I don't mean to sound grandiose. Nothing is that simple. I only held that space for about eighteen hours, but it got me thinking about what a world filled with people who knew ENOUGH might look like.

An Unexpected Space of ENOUGH

Am I really doing this?!!! I had to slap myself multiple times over, not out of joy but out of sheer disbelief. My daughter and I were boarding a four-day cruise to Mexico, and I never thought I would be standing there.

If you are a lover of cruises, you may find it hard to listen to what I am about to say. I HATE cruises. I am not a cruise person. I am a "sneak off into nature by yourself where it is just you and the trees, and you can be in peace" kind of gal. Or I'll delight in a pampering luxury space (still alone) where I don't have to talk or interact with anyone but where people are paid just to take care of me. I am (mostly) a vegetarian. I don't drink alcohol (I learned several decades ago it is not my friend). I like to be alone a lot. So, it is logical and reasonable for me to say I hate cruises. Still, up until that point, I had never been on one. But I knew cruises and I would clearly be a mismatch.

I kept surprising myself as we pulled our bags onto the ship. It was everything I had imagined in my nightmares: people drinking all day, loads of people hanging in the onboard casino, the cheesiest outfits, temptations to overeat at every buffet brimming with food, and more. And yet I really enjoyed myself. Sure, some of the enjoyment came from surprise aspects of the cruise I hadn't counted on: a small balcony where you could spend hours watching the huge ocean move by . . . yes! Happy nature girl. The fact that when I got up in the morning, and most of the ship was still sleeping, I could walk around the track on the top deck in peace. But those were the footnotes to my joy.

ENOUGH had decided to ride along in my bag, and she had opened my heart soooo wide to soooo much life, it was hard not to be happy at every single thing . . . like Joshua whom I met in line at the coffee shop only to discover we had a shared love of tea. He was an avid cruiser, having spent the last fifteen years going with the same group of adults as their way to get together . . . like Svitlana, our beautiful cabin attendant who poured pure love into everything she touched in our room, who was from the Ukraine and who had (in the previous year) lost seventeen family members to the war, whose six-year-old daughter was living with her mom in Bulgaria in a shelter with four other families, and who honored me with this personal sharing of herself during a morning hallway conversation while she waited for people to leave so she could tidy their cabins.

ENOUGH also shined her light on the vast array of massively wonderfully cheesy T-shirts that masses of people would wear to showcase their group belonging or humor: "Oh ship! It's cruise time." "Fabulous at 50: celebrate the birthday girl!" "The anchor won't weigh down this party!" "I like big boats, and I cannot lie." The list goes on and on . . . every color, every size. The ridiculousness brought me pure, unadulterated joy.

Then there was the time ENOUGH scared and surprised me. I had spent my morning walking on the promenade deck, internally criticizing a guy a deck below wearing a politically focused T-shirt and smoking a cigarette. Sitting from my throne on high, I felt comfortable in my judgments until he put out his cigarette, climbed the steps to my deck and struck up a conversation with me. We had a great, sweet, meaningful conversation about all the things that really matter in life. The conversation didn't last long, but it slapped me back into a reality where I lived my values instead of talking about them.

The trip filled me with more unexpected delights than I had anticipated—the flesh that unapologetically paraded out of swimsuits—flesh like mine loaded with cellulite but in all different colors and configurations. Bathing suits that were small, large, knit, and tight, baggy, and barely there. Humans of all shapes, colors, and sizes from different countries and all different walks of life—demonstrating that, despite the popular news, we *can* all get along. The last place I expected to find ENOUGH was on a cruise, but she continued to show me that her presence didn't rely on any people or any circumstances whatsoever. In her quiet grace, she broke all the rules.

I could go on and on. What changed? The cruise experience hadn't changed. It was almost exactly as I had anticipated. But I was there with a different traveler; ENOUGH showed me all of the joy and beauty that can exist in the strangest of places. She taught me to set down my judgments and go for the wealth I hungered for . . . the wealth of human connection, coming together, relaxing, and enjoying life. Now, I can't say my entire cruise experience was spent in bliss, far from it. But if you had told me I could love an experience like this, I would have told you that you were off your rocker.

What is possible? I know that ENOUGH has turned my acceptance and joy meter way up. Can ENOUGH turn our anger and irritation meter down and our compassion meter up?

These meaningful experiences kept adding up. I accumulated more and more wealth in my relationship with ENOUGH. She gave me hope about what was possible and helped me understand we had gotten it wrong all along.

Wrong All Along

I believe, in the end, we got the game wrong all along. Or at least I did. I can't speak for others. Somewhere, we bought into a framework, a world view, a way of living that put NOT ENOUGH front and center in all things. NOT ENOUGH played the charade of a bard telling us a tale of ourselves and our history, a long winding story that reinforced our belief in his sovereignty. We heard it long enough and strong enough that our world perspective warped. And now we believe that if we overthrow the king, we will starve.

How wrong we are.

If we took all of the extra food in the world and gave it to those who were hungry, poverty would be obliterated. Similarly, if we took only the excess money that exceeds what can be spent in certain people's lifetimes and redistributed it to those who have needs, financial need would be obliterated.

I'm not saying these are the right solutions or that solutions are simple. I am simply saying this very f*cking clearly: NOT ENOUGH incessantly sings us his narrative, but the story keeps us sleepwalking, wandering through our lives in a fog of our own making.

Another narrative is possible. Another's story screams, in her silence, to be told.

She definitely woke me up. I didn't plan to write about her at all. I don't feel qualified. I haven't lived with her for the number of years I feel it might take to develop the sort of expertise needed for a biography. But every time I tried to put her off, she was present. She didn't raise her voice or shout or yell. She didn't demand or force. For heaven's sake, she never even asked me to write this. Quite the opposite. She woke me up with her silent witness, a presence so profound I could not ignore her. She called to me through her embraces, given freely while expecting nothing in return. She laid her body down as a coat over the puddle of life to keep my feet dry. She spoke to me through my tears.

She touched me through the light in my heart. She walked into the most unlikely characters in my life's narrative to keep teaching me new lessons: lessons of hope, lessons of joy, lessons of peace, lessons of possibilities.

Even now, she keeps calling me. She tells me we have only just begun, that this story is just the start. She invites me to new adventures, new worlds, and new ways of being. I often try to reason with her rationally. She never disagrees. She simply opens another door.

She slides in on slipper wings, whispering a song we know by heart but forgot in a faraway dream, standing silent witness to our weariness . . . this never-ending, always enfolding, energy source of hope and dreams and possibilities . . . clearing tunnels and tracks, breaking bars and barriers to allow all joy and flow . . . her earnest presence births, bubbles, and overflows with her message. You are enough! There is enough! You have enough. *Feel me,* she says without words and then gently wraps her arms around me. I try to resist her. I try to run, hit, and destroy her, but she persists in her presence.

Her vulnerability and stillness are her strengths, the source of her power. It is through her that I experience—that I feel and love and laugh and cry and care and live. Because ENOUGH is where my fierceness exists, where my power lies. And you may dismiss her or overlook her or pass her up, but you cannot, may not, do not have the power to erase her. Her softness may make you uncomfortable because it reflects back to you all of the things you long for but are afraid to know. I understand how peculiar this is, how wildly unexpected that I built a living-breathing-expressing, altar-like monument to ENOUGH.

How did this come to be? How am I able to deny the proof of the multitude of moments? How did I come to promote this always-deepening truth? The reality of it? How did I come to draw her in, seek her out, and desperately share her over and over? She continues to whisper gently, softly, over and over and over . . . until finally, in quiet resignation, her voices are me.

I AM ENOUGH.

ACKNOWLEDGMENTS

To Eric, Brian, and Neva, my beautiful family, who have taught me the raw joy, beauty, messiness, and power of fierce loving.

To all my guides on this plane and others. Thank you for reminding me that the job of the heart doesn't end on earth. Thank you to Laura for bringing them more fully into my life each and every week.

To Nicole, I may never find the words to express my gratitude for your unconditional belief in me. We don't need public pages for expression, but I know you know your space in my heart.

To my board of directors, Ela, Kathy, Michele, and Wendy, my fellow magic makers. Our meetings, where words became spells, wove a fabric of titanium belief in me.

To Denise, Edda, Gertrude—friends forged through fire, fair witnesses to life's wonders and weariness—thank you for your constant and ever-unfolding friendships.

To Caryn, for converting coffee shops into churches, spaces for worship and wonder, embracing both the joy and humility of being human.

To Stacey, Sanjida, Ruth, Phil, Munzoor, Marilyn, Laura T, Kiki, Kate, Jillian, Jayme, Deb, Beryl, Amy, Alison, and so many others who walked with me, listened to me, revealed themselves to me, broke bread with me, supported me, and became the permaculture and ecosystem of my life.

To all the authors who didn't even know they were on my journey of support—Rachel Rodgers, Anita Moorjani, Sonya Renee Taylor, Amanda Frances, Suzanne Simard, Sy Montgomery, Adrienne Maree Brown, John O'Donohue, Paramahansa Yogananda, and so many more.

To all the spaces and people that served as the birthplaces of this work, particularly my friends at Cupitol Café and Eli Tea.

To my many clients who are truly my teachers. Thank you for letting me talk to myself through you.

---

www.ingramcontent.com/pod-product-compliance
Lightning Source LLC
Chambersburg PA
CBHW070122260726
48658CB00001B/228